Sermons Together

Scott Taylor

Parson's Porch Books
www.parsonsporchbooks.com

Sermons Together
ISBN: Softcover 978-1-951472-48-1
Copyright © 2020 by Scott Taylor

All rights reserved. No part of this book may be reproduced or transmitted in any form or by any means, electronic or mechanical, including photocopying, recording, or by any information storage and retrieval system, without permission in writing from the publisher.

Sermons Together

Contents

Acknowledgements 9

Introduction 11

We're Not In Kansas Anymore, Toto 13
 Isaiah 6:1-8

Once Upon A Time 18
 Genesis 18:1-15

We're Off To See The Wizard... 23
 Acts 1:1-8

Don't They Know Who I Am?! 29
 Luke 17:5-10

God, Thank You, But... 35
 Luke 18:9-14

A Never Ending Buffet 39
 John 4:5-42

It's Just A Baby Boy 44
 Matthew 2:13-23

My Child, My Beloved 49
 Matthew 3: 13-17

A Pretty Fishy Story 53
 Matthew 4:12-23

Blazing Glory? Or Stewardship? 56
 Matthew 17:1-9

Saved From Ourselves 60
 John 3:1-17

A Solitary Shell Game 65
 John 9:1-41

What's Death Got To Do With It? 70
 John 11:1-45

See, It's Like This... 76
 Matthew 21:1-11; Psalm 118:1-2, 19-29

Listen to the Cross	82
Psalm 22:1-2, 23-24	
You Can't Keep A Good Man Down	86
Matthew 28:1-10	
The Price of Violence	92
Gen 6:9-22, 7:24, 8:14-19	
Promises Kept	97
Genesis 21:1-7	
An Impossible Request	102
Genesis 22:1-14	
Thin Spaces	107
Genesis 28:10-19a	
Be Prepared	111
Matthew 25:1-13	
A Letter from Home	115
Gal 6:7-16	
The Illusion of Salvation	121
Luke 23:33-43	
The Sound of Giving	127
Matthew 6:1-4	
Little Is - As Little Does	131
Luke 19:1-10	
Oceans of Hope	136
Luke 21:5-19	
Guess Who's Coming For Dinner?	144
Luke 14:15-24	
What if?	149
Mark 6:32-44	
Spiritual Freedom	157
Gal 5:1, 13-25	

My God, Your God 159
    Acts 11:1-18
Shouting Stones 161
    Luke 19:28-40
Sin In A Nutshell 163
    Luke 4:1-11

Acknowledgements

When I preach, I often start with a paraphrased prayer from Psalm 19:4: "O Lord, may the words of my mouth and the mediations of our hearts together be acceptable to You, our rock and our Redeemer." Silently to myself, I add a second prayer: "O God, you better speak through me 'because I have no clue what to say!" I need to thank God, first and foremost, for backing me up all these years with an answer to that prayer. I have always found that when I can let go and let Spirit enter, preaching goes well and I am deeply thankful for that help. Thank you, God, thank you.

I also want to thank all the professors and classmates and peers who have given me example after example to follow. In like manner, renowned preachers like Sharon Watkins, Barbara Brown Taylor, Fred Craddock, William Barber II, Rick Lowery, Chuck Shorow, Bill Inglish and on and on gave me awe-inspiring, challenging, and beautifully moving examples to emulate even if I never reached their pinnacle of excellence.

Since the essence of preaching is communication, every preacher understands that the congregations who listened and shared the sermon experience deserve a special thank you for their attentiveness and patience. Thank you especially to the communities of Disciples Christian Church, Bartlesville, OK and First Christian Church, Grand Island, NE for our years together.

Finally, I must thank my wife, Patty, for her grace and patience while I focused on exegesis and writing. Her love means everything and simply saying 'thank you' seems a paltry effort in light of her herculean devotion to this late-in-life pastor. Thank you all!

Rev. Dr. Scott Taylor
Bartlesville, OK

Introduction

This is not a text to teach the art of preaching nor to share any exegetical or hermeneutical technique; it is a simple collection of sermons preached over the years from 2005-2020. As I began to consider putting this together, I was first daunted with the size of the task required to fashion all of these sermons into good prose. No one has enough time to do that. Upon reflection, I have decided to leave the sermons pretty much as written save for minor editing to fix typos, misspellings, etc. No major editing has been done; the sermons are basically just as prepared and delivered.

Since preaching is an oral form of communication, it is also a form of performance, just as a piece of theater or a movie. It requires the same elements those do; it requires timing and good vocal projection and planning. Humor is a useful tool and it is important to offer consolation, i.e., while some husbands may beat their wives, not all husbands do so and it is good to offer that so as not to put all the men in the audience on the spot! I have found it very helpful to put cues or directions in the sermon to aid me in delivering it. Some of these will be self-evident - [*pause*] means to intentionally pause at that point, for example. I have used bracketed text as a directive throughout my sermons. Additionally, it may be noted that I have a lot of exclamation points and dashes. Exclamation points remind me to accentuate certain statements while dashes signify a short pause. On occasion, I have used italicized text to remind me to emphasize a point or to note a repeating theme that I want to highlight. In the end, preaching has two key actors - the preacher and the congregation; they need to work well together.

I make note of these performance cues so that anyone who wants to use these sermons should understand that they may need to alter them to fit their own performance style.

I have tried to select sermons that were well-received and remembered. For example, in "God, Thank You, But…," I first used the phrase 'bless their hearts' as a marker for when we try to wash away our judgementalism. Even today, many years later, members will say 'bless their heart' to point to such mean-spirited language! If I'm honest, I believe it has been said, "Pastor Scott means well but, bless his heart…" which gives this preacher the corollary concern, be careful what you say as it will come back to you!

The majority of these sermons are fully written out including any illustrations that I would have presented from memory much as any storyteller would. However, many of my sermons were presented from a simple outline format. I could print the outline on a single side of paper that could be conveniently folded and placed in the cover of my Bible for easy reference as I preached. This allowed me to move away from the pulpit and into the congregation for a more personal approach. I have included four examples of sermons in outline form and I believe it will be clear how these could be fleshed out extemporaneously.

In the end, the message God wants God's people to hear will be met by sincere preaching as well as deep listening. I suppose it might even be parabolic: God's message is like a parrot offering its best oration as listeners grin and catch a word or two. I hope that these sermons bless you as my listeners blessed me over the years.

We're Not In Kansas Anymore, Toto
Isaiah 6:1-8

6 In the year that King Uzziah died, I saw the Lord sitting on a throne, high and lofty; and the hem of his robe filled the temple. 2 Seraphs were in attendance above him; each had six wings: with two they covered their faces, and with two they covered their feet, and with two they flew. 3 And one called to another and said: "Holy, holy, holy is the Lord of hosts; the whole earth is full of his glory." 4 The pivots on the thresholds shook at the voices of those who called, and the house filled with smoke. 5 And I said: "Woe is me! I am lost, for I am a man of unclean lips, and I live among a people of unclean lips; yet my eyes have seen the King, the Lord of hosts!" 6 Then one of the seraphs flew to me, holding a live coal that had been taken from the altar with a pair of tongs. 7 The seraph touched my mouth with it and said: "Now that this has touched your lips, your guilt has departed and your sin is blotted out." 8 Then I heard the voice of the Lord saying, "Whom shall I send, and who will go for us?" And I said, "Here am I; send me!"

As I drove across Kansas Thursday afternoon, I must admit that I spent most of the time just trying to catch my breath and get ready for the next spin of the whirlwind that is moving an entire household out of the old place, closing on a new home, and moving that entire household into the new place - in one week!

We made it! - But not without trials and tribulations; not without doubts.

Moving is such an upsetting event, isn't it? We had everything in its place and we knew where that 'place' was - well, maybe I didn't always know - but my wife, Patty, knew where everything's 'place' was. Now everything still has its place - it just happens to be in a box at the moment. By the way, if any of you need boxes, why, I happen to have more than a few you can have...

So, we made it! Well, Gracie the cat and I have made it - Patty's down in Lubbock on a family reunion trip that had been planned 6 months ago. I'm still trying to work out how she managed to set that up so that she didn't have to deal with finishing all the packing and loading and then unloading! But I always knew she was a bright and creative lady - she knew what she was doing. But she's had doubts and trials and tribulations, too - which - I'm sure she'll be happy to share when she gets here tomorrow! You know, I'll bet you've had doubts too.

Now I know we all know intellectually that we cannot know the future, but mostly, we can avoid looking at that fact and 'pretend' we know what's going to happen in the future. I've even got my calendar with me at all times [*hold up iPhone*] so I can tell you if I've got anything scheduled on whatever day you care to know about. I can check the weather too and tell you if it'll be raining next week. But in this move, that charade falls apart and then the doubts and fears creep in.

And that, my new friends, reminds me of a tale about a priest who spent his entire life in the shadow of the Matterhorn. He loved the outdoors and longed to climb the Matterhorn - someday. Well, finally, he retired and 'someday' came and the little priest could 'see' his future; he could see himself standing proudly on the summit. And it happened - he did climb the mountain and he did stand on the very top and shout, "I did it!" And then he slipped and fell over the edge! With certain death close at hand, he blindly reached out and grabbed a twisted little branch of a tree on the side of the cliff. Hanging by one arm, emptiness below him for 2000 feet, his grasp of the future all but gone, he cried out, "O God, help me!" [*pause*] And a deep voice seemed to come from everywhere at once saying, "Do not fear; let go and I will be with you." The little priest, looked around, and whispered in a shaky voice, "Is there anybody else there?" You see? It's hard to trust and have faith when your future is uncertain. Like it is when you're moving.

But we made it! We 'let go and let God', as the saying goes. We did not fear but put our trust and hope in God, the one who cares for us and whose we are.

This is what the people faced in Isaiah's time; this was God's message that Isaiah carried to the people, "Do not fear." But they didn't listen; it's hard to trust and have faith when your future is uncertain. You see, this was the time of the Syro-Ephraimite war. The Assyrians under Tiglath-pilaster were threatening from the north so Israel and Syria formed a coalition against Assyria - and tried to get Judah to join in. When King Ahaz refused, they attacked the southern Kingdom of Judah. Isaiah comes forth in this situation to tell Ahaz, in a nutshell, "Hang tight with God; do not fear 'these two smoldering stumps of firebrands." But Ahaz didn't listen; he formed an alliance with Assyria making Judah a vassal to Assyria to get protection. In the end, though, the Assyrians wiped out Syria and the northern Kingdom, Israel, and in 722 BCE, brought the northern kingdom to an end. It didn't buy Judah much; they were taken into Babylonian exile not long afterward.

It's hard to trust and have faith when your future is uncertain.

So why did we move - if it's fraught with so much trouble? Whatever could make someone move away from everything familiar, from family and home and safety and that facade of a sure future? God can.

That brings us to today's text, which I've so conveniently avoided so far! This particular text in Isaiah is often described as 'the call of Isaiah' but it's actually a commissioning of sorts. It's Isaiah's call to deliver God's message to the people of God. And what an amazing scene! The passage starts by dating itself: "in the year that King Uzziah died," that's 736/735 BCE. And immediately, it goes on to make it clear that Isaiah found himself in the holy court - "I saw the Lord sitting on a throne, high and lofty" and "Seraphs were in attendance saying, "Holy, holy, holy is YHWH of hosts; the whole earth is full of his glory!"

Seraphs talk that way. The HarperCollins Bible Dictionary says, "seraphim - fiery beings of supernatural origin. The etymology of the Hebrew word, seraphim, suggests a translation of 'fiery ones' and probably stems from the fiery imagery often associated with the Presence of God."[1] So it was not hard for Isaiah to recognize he was in peril - he cries out, "Woe is me! I am lost, for I am a man of unclean lips, and I live among a people of unclean lips; yet my eyes have seen the King, YHWH of hosts!"

It's dangerous to be in the presence of YHWH - everybody knows this. All we have to do is go back to that earlier call story of Moses at the burning bush (again - fiery) in Exodus 3:4 and 5. "When YHWH saw that he had turned aside, He called to him out of the bush, "Moses, Moses!" And Moses said, "Here I am." Then YHWH said, "Come no closer! Remove the sandals from your feet, for the place on which you are standing is holy ground." Now, this is just a fiery bush - not the Lord with his garment hem filling the whole place and seraphim flying about - no wonder Isaiah's scared!

But in a marvelous ritual, one of the seraphs takes a burning, i.e., fiery, coal from the altar and touches Isaiah's lips with it to remove his guilt and sin. Then Isaiah hears the voice of God saying, "Whom shall I send, and who will go for us?" Isaiah answered, "Here am I; send me!"

Whom shall I send, and who will go for us?

These are questions that are familiar and frightening to me - and to congregations - for we've heard them, too.

    [*pause*]

It's a funny thing, this whole search and call process we ministers and search committees go through. It's very easy to fall into the mistaken belief that it's basically a job search. And actually, it starts out in a very similar way. It started by me, AKA 'the minister', filling out what is known as a 'ministerial profile'.

Basically, this is a resume - just a lot more than 2 pages! Once that and a few legal details were taken care of, my 'papers' were made available throughout the regions I selected. Not being at all sure, this being my first try at 'search and call', I said "Go ahead and send them everywhere!"

Then, slowly at first, I got some phone calls from churches looking for ministers, asking if I would like to be considered. Basically, this is the "We'll send you our papers if you send us yours" phase. It's like going through the car lot scoping out the cars, kicking a few tires, finding the ones that seem to be a possibility. And realistically, that's pretty much it in the beginning. But then something strange happened and without noticing when or how, I woke up and realized, "We're not in Kansas anymore, Toto!"

It happened during a simple phone conversation. Now, to start with, I need to make something perfectly clear. When I graduated from Phillips Theological Seminary, my first thought was not, "Boy, I hope someone in Nebraska calls me!" Nope, I was looking much closer to home for starters. I had a sense of some good opportunities with churches right around Tulsa so I wasn't looking too far away.

But hey, I'll talk to anybody, right? Maybe the Holy Spirit will call from who knows where - hey, it could happen! Yeah, right. So let me tell you about your Search committee. They, too, had their moments of doubt and trials and tribulations. They, too, couldn't help but find some aspects of the whole search and call process to be like an employee search. But I know they also had their own "We're not in Kansas anymore, Toto!" moment. It started like all the other interviews. The chairperson called me and asked if I'd be interested in interviewing for the position of minister here at First Christian Church and I said, "Sure, I'd love to talk to you." We selected a time and date and made our polite goodbyes and hung up, whereupon I immediately went to Yahoo maps to figure out just where in the world Grand Island, Nebraska was!

I got your church profile papers - your resume - and thought it looked interesting - keeping an open mind and all, you understand. Then we had our first phone interview - and something happened. It was no longer simply about a job - we had entered a holy space and time - and we all knew it. I remember telling Patty after the interview that it was the best first interview, I'd had with anyone - and by that time, I'd been through 4 initial interviews and was into my 2nd and third interviews with several churches. But something was different - we weren't in Kansas anymore.

And that only became more evident with each passing day. The Search Committee called me the very next day to arrange a time for me to come to Grand Island and visit in person. As an off-hand remark, I mentioned that while we'd picked a date in mid-July, we weren't really doing anything on the 4th-6th so could come then... and, after a pause, the chairperson said softly, "That's what we were hoping for!" You see, we weren't in Kansas anymore, Toto.

I wish I could tell you we all saw a burning bush. I wish I could describe the seraphim singing 'Holy, Holy, Holy! as Isaiah did so eloquently - but that's not what I saw or heard. What I heard was meant for me and spoken to me in a moment of deep, deep spirit that I won't soon forget. After sharing a meal together, I sat facing your - whole - search - committee. And they, almost as one, looked at me and said, "We have prayed and searched. We have listened for God's direction, and we believe God has sent you to us. We would like you to be our new minister."

But there, deeply within all of us in that moment, I heard God calling to me, "Whom shall I send, and who will go for us?"

I want to - no, I need to assure you - this was no mere job offer. This was a call to me - and through me to all of us - to go where God leads us, to go where God needs us, to go in spite of the doubts and trials and tribulations. God is calling us, saying, "Do not fear!"

And I have answered, on behalf of all of us, "Here am I, send me!"

May it be so always. Amen.

[1] Sweeney, Marvin A. in *HarperCollins Bible Dictionary*, Paul J. Achtemeier, general ed., (New York, NY: HaperCollins), 1996, p. 998.

Once Upon A Time
Genesis 18:1-15

18 The Lord appeared to Abraham by the oaks of Mamre, as he sat at the entrance of his tent in the heat of the day. 2 He looked up and saw three men standing near him. When he saw them, he ran from the tent entrance to meet them, and bowed down to the ground. 3 He said, "My lord, if I find favor with you, do not pass by your servant. 4 Let a little water be brought, and wash your feet, and rest yourselves under the tree. 5 Let me bring a little bread, that you may refresh yourselves, and after that you may pass on—since you have come to your servant." So they said, "Do as you have said." 6 And Abraham hastened into the tent to Sarah, and said, "Make ready quickly three measures of choice flour, knead it, and make cakes." 7 Abraham ran to the herd, and took a calf, tender and good, and gave it to the servant, who hastened to prepare it. 8 Then he took curds and milk and the calf that he had prepared and set it before them; and he stood by them under the tree while they ate.

9 They said to him, "Where is your wife Sarah?" And he said, "There, in the tent." 10 Then one said, "I will surely return to you in due season, and your wife Sarah shall have a son." And Sarah was listening at the tent entrance behind him. 11 Now Abraham and Sarah were old, advanced in age; it had ceased to be with Sarah after the manner of women. 12 So Sarah laughed to herself, saying, "After I have grown old, and my husband is old, shall I have pleasure?" 13 The Lord said to Abraham, "Why did Sarah laugh, and say, 'Shall I indeed bear a child, now that I am old?' 14 Is anything too wonderful for the Lord? At the set time I will return to you, in due season, and Sarah shall have a son." 15 But Sarah denied, saying, "I did not laugh"; for she was afraid. He said, "Oh yes, you did laugh."

Isn't this a marvelous story? It's full of twists and turns and surprises and odd details. There's humor; there's a surprising God who gives away the ability to listen to us even when we think we're only talking to ourselves. But Abraham and Sarah going to have a child at their age? I mean come on, that can't be fact - but it's true - deep down true.

You see, that's what stories are. Stories are always full of interpretation and nuance and distance and - color! That's what makes them great, that's why we love novels. They may not be factual but they say something deep down true that resonates in us. Here, I'll show you what I mean. I spent a delightful time this week with Mother Gerry and her daughter, Jane. Gerry was telling us how she was able to get back to her beloved bridge game earlier that afternoon and it came out that Jane somehow never picked up the bridge bug, so to speak. And then this story came out: Jane said, "It's because you played so much and I had to sit in the corner and be quiet... sit in the corner as you played for hours and I got nothing but a glass of water and a toothpick!"

I know, I know! That's terrible! But *they* were both smiling. You see? That's not factual - but it's got a deep down truth that mother and daughter share that takes them back to those days and I'm sure as sure can be that they both smell the coffee and the see the colors in the room from way back then whenever they retell this story. That's another characteristic of good stories - we never tire of telling and listening to them. They need to be told and retold. They may not be factual - but they're true!

Like our story today - it's for sure true and we know it 'cause it's our story too!

For you see, we have a story to tell - we have a story to tell, too. But let's look at this exciting story first. Biblical stories are amazing in their precision and sharp ways of leading us to these truths and I love the way this one starts. The very first thing we learn is, "YHWH appeared to Abraham by the oaks of Mamre, as he sat at the entrance of his tent in the heat of the day." This is really sneaky - this is the narrator talking! We're being let in on the secret - Abraham doesn't know it's YHWH - but we do! He's sitting there under the big oak tree, a light breeze is rustling the leaves making that soothing 'wwhhsssshhhh' sound that makes a nap feel real good, and the shade feels cool against hot sun beating down on the dusty road just beyond Abraham's feet. Abraham's just nodding - and his head jerks up - you know how it does when you're trying to stay awake - and not succeeding? There's three men standing there. He didn't see them coming, they're just there.

And then he does an amazing thing. He jumps up to greet these three strangers! Would you have done that? I think I'd've been scared or at least embarrassed at being caught out in a nap. But Abraham, no, he jumps right up to welcome them. Now there must've been something special about these men too because Abraham greets them as a servant saying, "My Lord, if I find favor with you, do not pass by your servant. Let a little water be brought, and wash your feet, and rest yourselves under the tree. Let me bring you a little bread that you may refresh yourselves, and after that you may pass on - since you have come to your servant." It's easy - too easy - for us to jump to the conclusion that Abraham knows this is God. But we only know that because the narrator told us so! Abraham doesn't know this - no one's told him. But he responds with a gracious hospitality because somehow, Abraham knows everyone's a messenger for God.

That kind of hospitality to the stranger was understood in ancient times though. It's at the heart of Exodus 23:9, "You shall not oppress a resident alien; you know the heart of an alien, for you were aliens in the land of Egypt." , an admonition that will be a reminder to the Israelites to show hospitality like patriarchal Abraham did. And what hospitality! Three measures don't sound like much to us because we think in terms of *our* measures - cups - but the storyteller's talking about something on the order of 50 lbs. here! And a whole calf! This is way over the top extravagant - why, it's like... a buffalo feed, maybe. Naw...it couldn't be that extravagant, could it?

And then the amazing conclusion - totally impossible, Abraham and Sarah having a child at their age. Why, it's not only impossible but downright scandalous! Except for God. And God doesn't even see it as scandalous, no, YHWH says, "Is anything too *wonderful* for YHWH? Wonderful - yes, a child is a wonderful creation. And then the delightful - or scary, depending on how you look at it - revelation of a sneaky God who can listen even to our thoughts and innermost feelings. Just when Sarah thinks she's all alone, God whispers, "Oh yes, you did laugh!"

What a great story - we should tell this one again and again! But we've got a story to tell, too. You know, I'm starting to visit everyone and, although I've only scratched the surface, I've heard some great stories. Here's one: I've wondered since I first visited here why the front of the church faces east when all the traffic is on the west side and almost all of us enter from the west side. Then it was pointed out to me that when the church was built - it was out in the country! Everything faced east because there was nothing but cornfields to the west. What I like about that is the way you built way out here where you might welcome the strangers passing by. The Gregersens, who live just around the corner on Sherman street, said the same thing. Their home looked over fields when they moved there in 1965.

Stories. I heard some great ones about the way you love to gather around the table and share a meal. Volney Lofgreen told me how he and Dr. Cunningham started the Buffalo Feed around 1960. The very next year, you invited all the men of the district and it grew to become the best attended men's program in the entire state! 'Let a little water be brought, and wash your feet, and rest yourselves under the tree. Let me bring you a little bread - a little buffalo - that you may refresh yourselves...'

The CWF found the same spirit of hospitality and abundance when the Feast of the Booths Bazaar was first held in October of 1968. Marcela Williams has been here since, well, forever, I think, and she shared with me how the Bazaar

was founded to bring people together and to worship God - and it still is today! The women involved in the Bazaar have always understood the extravagance of '3 measures' - I understand that literally hundreds of pounds of noodles were made each year! Now, I know that's one tradition that's changed as some of the cooks have retired and gotten beyond the noodle making age, but I'm going to step up and join the tradition by making some noodles - maybe just one measure - for the next Bazaar! [*pause*] 'Let a little water be brought, and wash your feet, and rest yourselves under the tree. Let me bring you a little bread - some noodles - that you may refresh yourselves...
'

And there's other examples of great meals - the Circle 4 prime rib dinner, the salad dinner, the men's monthly breakfast, the monthly gathering after worship, the ice cream social, and too many more to digest! I have been here just 2 and a half weeks - and, counting the retreat, I have shared 9 meals with you, in one form or another - if I add the meals we shared together during my visits in July and August, the total goes to 14!

'Let a little water be brought, and wash your feet, and rest yourselves under the tree. Let me bring you a little bread that you may refresh yourselves... 'Oh yes, we know this story - and we've got a story to tell, too.

It's not just about food here at First Christian Church, there are so many other stories. Volney shared with me how when he was minister here, you had the second largest Youth Group in the state - and Volney was a counselor or director at over 40 summer church camps. That's a lot of years of sitting under that oak tree and finding strangers at one's doorstep!! But I think my favorite story from Volney and Betty is how they surprised all of you when they got married. They managed to keep it a secret until that Sunday but then it was shared as a joy - and the whole congregation applauded and stood up in joy and happiness! You not only welcome the stranger; you take care of each other too. Bill and Betty Jussel shared with me how the Gregersens helped them when their lives were turned upside down. You have a deep love for your church and for your community.

Of course, it's not all serious and it's not all about helping in times of trouble. You share laughter and even some highjinks. Why, I heard that a young Bob Fickes was known to send paper airplanes flying from the balcony at the old church on 3rd St. - I'm not sure I should share this but... I hear he was even seen swinging from the balcony on occasion! Bill White told me about Ron and Linda Allen going around to visit everyone when they first came to the church, just as I'm doing now. He recalls inviting them to dinner only to learn that Linda, at least, was vegetarian! He filled me in on how Linda wanted

Ron to be vegetarian too - but whenever he was off on his own, he'd head for a big mac or a ham sandwich! I wonder - did Ron Allen or Bob Fickes ever deny these tales? And did they hear God whispering, "Oh yes, I heard you!"

Of course, there's also the story of the bat and the singing soprano. Ohh, you've 'heard' this one? Talk about a congregation wanting to help the stranger, the visitor, the alien in your midst! The way I hear it, every time the bat flew by the singer, she'd duck, never missing a beat - and the whole congregation would duck too! In sympathy, I suppose - or maybe fear. In either case, you were there with her all the way!

And I like the hidden stories. Have any of you met Lavina and Florence? These sisters come to the church every Wednesday morning and settle themselves into the Fellowship hall, one at one table and the other sort of cati-corner at an adjacent table. Armed with scotch-tape and patience, they carefully fold each newsletter and prepare it for mailing. I know they do this because I met them and visited with them last Wednesday. But did you know they've been doing this for - over - 20 - years? That speaks to a deep love for your church and for your community.

Yes, we've got a story to tell.

At the retreat yesterday, we shared meals and fellowship but we also told our stories to each other. I heard how Scott Horne and Kevin Fickes spent many enjoyable days at Kamp Kaleo - how they were the fastest across the lagoon - and how the camp directors wanted them to be in separate cabins some years! And I know I've just scratched the surface of learning your stories. I've started to visit but I've got lots of visiting yet to do. Don't worry, I still plan on visiting everyone - I want to hear those stories.

You see now, don't you? Stories help us identify who - and whose - we are. Even when we know a story isn't necessarily factual, we know it's true - deep down true. Like the story of Abraham and Sarah - we know that story - because it's our story too! It's a story of real people with limitations being intertwined with the story of our God where nothing is impossible. And if that story is our story, then maybe the story we share around this communion table is our story too. The story of a love so great it surpasses death and time, a story of redemption - is our story too.

Boy, have we got a story to tell!

May it be always true!

We're Off to See the Wizard...
Acts 1:1-8

1 In the first book, Theophilus, I wrote about all that Jesus did and taught from the beginning 2 until the day when he was taken up to heaven, after giving instructions through the Holy Spirit to the apostles whom he had chosen. 3 After his suffering he presented himself alive to them by many convincing proofs, appearing to them during forty days and speaking about the kingdom of God. 4 While staying with them, he ordered them not to leave Jerusalem, but to wait there for the promise of the Father. "This," he said, "is what you have heard from me; 5 for John baptized with water, but you will be baptized with the Holy Spirit not many days from now."

6 So when they had come together, they asked him, "Lord, is this the time when you will restore the kingdom to Israel?" 7 He replied, "It is not for you to know the times or periods that the Father has set by his own authority. 8 But you will receive power when the Holy Spirit has come upon you; and you will be my witnesses in Jerusalem, in all Judea and Samaria, and to the ends of the earth."

In that classic movie, "The Wizard of Oz," the four main characters have been through all sorts of trouble. Dorothy (and Toto) got sucked up into a tornado, the Tim Man rusted up out in the forest, the Scarecrow was being picked on by the crows...and the Lion had lost his nerve, his courage. But they found a common goal in all of their stories and, armed with enthusiasm and grit and determination, they assembled, ready to take on the world. Arm in arm, they stepped out in that famous song and skipping dance, "We're off to see the wizard, the wonderful wizard of Oz - because, because, because, because, because...because of the wonderful things he does!" For some reason, that's always been a favorite movie for me - heck, I even learned how to do that little skipping number!

So anyway, they were heading off into the unknown in high style alright! They knew where they were going and they knew what would happen when they got there. Or, at least they thought they did. Of course, we know the rest of the story; we know about their trials and tribulations, and about how it's all about sticking with your friends and family and what you knew all along. What did Dorothy say when she awoke back in Kansas? "There's no place like home...there's no place like home." She'd thought she had to go someplace else to be complete but then she discovered everything she needed was right there at home all along. As the storyteller might say, "and they lived happily ever after!"

Well, I suppose that could happen, but the uncertainty of an unknown future is more likely.

The characters in our text today face such a dilemma. They've been through harrowing - no, terrifying - times. Their leader, the one they called "Messiah", died on a cross. Well, that's what they heard since they'd all fled. But shucks, everybody knows no one gets crucified and lives! But then, amazingly, impossibly, there he is - alive again! Yet just when they get used to Jesus being back with them, he leaves! What a dilemma! What do they do now? We face the same dilemma. It's the ages-old dilemma - where do we go from here? Dorothy and her friends faced it; the disciples faced it; you've faced it with each change in your ministers over the past 7 years; and I faced it the day after graduation.

Where - do we go - from here?

Well, thankfully, our text today gives us some good direction, a path we can follow. It may not be a 'yellow brick road', but it's still a way for us to go. That's what we'll do this morning - see if our text can give us some clues as we wrestle with the question - where do we go from here?

Of course, I suppose the first thing to note in the text is how the disciples still can't grasp the idea that God's kingdom isn't about earthly power. Their primary question, as reported by this author, is "Lord, is this the time when you will restore the kingdom to Israel?" Jesus snipes back, "It's not for you to know the times or periods that the Father has set by his own authority." He does kind of soften this though by adding, "But you will receive power when the Holy Spirit has come upon you;.." Isn't that just the way we are? We'll say we're ready for a journey, we're ready to face the world but, yo, God...could you give us some special powers? Maybe have a radioactive spider bite us or maybe we'll get powers like those 'Heroes' on TV. It's hard to know what sort of power Jesus is talking about but there's a clear implication it's not the same sort of power the disciples are hoping for!

So I looked up the greek term used here. The overarching definition is 'inherent power, power residing in a thing by virtue of its nature, or which a person or thing exerts and puts forth'. In this specific case though, it's really 'under or full of the power of the Holy Spirit, or by the power and influence of the Holy Spirit'. It's also specifically used in Acts as the power of performing miracles, every kind of power of working miracles'. Which is a good thing for the very next thing Jesus says is his prime directive to the disciples. He says, "and you will be witnesses of me both in Jerusalem, and in all Judea, and Samaria, and unto the ends of the earth." I think that means even to Nebraska and beyond!

Do you see? Somehow, 'power' and 'witnessing' are tied together. 'Witnesses of me' Jesus says. [*big sigh*] Well, back to the greek! Here, the term 'witnesses' means 'to affirm that one has seen or heard or experienced something'. In the New Testament it's said of the apostles - 'as those who had been eye and ear witnesses of the extraordinary sayings, deeds, and sufferings of Jesus'. In general, it means 'to give testimony'.

Now, it's getting clearer, isn't it?!

So this is the last advice or call or direction that Jesus gives the disciples and, by way of 2000 years of tradition, us. In a nutshell - "You'll have the power of the Holy Spirit to help you - now go everywhere and be my witnesses. Testify to what I have said and done."

Well, that's all well and good - if you're an apostle! Or even if you're Paul who saw the same risen Christ the Apostles saw. But what about us? What are we going to testify to?

What - are *we* - going to testify to?

[*pause*]

When I put together the outline for my Ordination service 6 months ago, I called it 'A Celebration of Journey'. And I picked out a nice picture of a road leading off into the distance, clearly beckoning for a journey. I thought it was a good picture. Little did I know how the Holy Spirit might use that moment. For you see, that service was in May - long before I heard from the Search Committee, long before I ever thought of coming to Nebraska. Yet look at the picture I selected - the road goes through - cornfields! It is my witness that this call was meant to be - even way back before you or I gave it any thought.

What else can I witness to? Well, Jesus said over and over that we should take care of each other; we should take care of the poor and sick and homeless. One Sunday morning, several years ago, we were going through our normal prayer time in the worship service and I was praying a prayer I've said many times. I prayed, "God, thank you for the abundance you've given me - give some of it to someone who needs it more than I do as I have plenty." I've prayed that prayer many times as a prayer of thanks and a prayer of request. But something happened differently this particular morning. As I was praying 'give some of what I've got 'cause I've got plenty…', a voice came into my head and whispered, "No, that's why I gave it to you."

Here we are in the Fall - the normal time for Stewardship messages and boy, that was one for me! And I can witness that as a result of that encounter, I started to tithe - not because it was the right thing to do but because I had plenty. And sure enough, when I gave more, I still had plenty! I can testify to that. I can testify that giving brings unexpected gains and gifts just like Jesus said it would.

I can testify to the healing power of Jesus' message. I have been around many, many people in recovery from various forms of addiction and I have seen families that were torn apart reconcile and become whole again. I have seen lives that were shattered, and people who were in hell right here, right now - shine with redemption and forgiveness.

I have seen a man afflicted with blindness due to AIDS rejoice at new friendships because he no longer saw race or gender or sexual identity or age - he saw brothers and sisters - all children of God. I have witnessed Jesus' non-judgmental love among the lepers of our society, those people who are HIV positive. I have witnessed how coming together in a loving community who did not judge them gave them strength and hope - and life - beyond all reasonable expectations.

I have witnessed teenagers - who are so busy you have to schedule things months in advance - go on a mission trip and work in pouring rain to fix a home that had been nearly destroyed by Hurricane Rita. I saw those same kids work in South Houston despite their realistic fears about the 'hood'. I heard them ask for work to do; I heard them tell me that doing mission work was more meaningful to them than even going to the Fiesta Texas theme park in San Antonio.

And more recently, I have witnessed a retreat where people who've had a hard go of the tough times First Christian Church has seen over the years, come alive with renewed hope and energy. I saw how a few fish and loaves turned into a feast! I heard people share deeply and saw tears of new life as we let our vision sweep us into the future. All because Jesus showed us a new way to love each other, to care for each other, to be in community together.

And just this very week, I saw people respond to Jesus' message of love in community by coming to our first Monday Noon Prayer group. We sent cards out to those we prayed for and we have already heard from several of those people who felt a deeper connection to this community as a result.

[*pause*]

It's hard to imagine what it felt like to the disciples to be told 'you will be witnesses of me' but at least they had the actual experience of having seen and heard Jesus. What do we do? Where do we go? Those of us so far removed from the living Jesus.

Or are we so far removed? Our testimony today is certainly just as powerful a witness as anyone who's gone before us. In fact, it is *our* continuing faith and witness that makes their earlier faith real.

The Thursday evening Bible Study is in the Letter to the Hebrews right now, and the hearers of that letter faced this very same issue - where do we go from here? They get the same admonition - the climax is right there in Hebrews 12:1-2: "Therefore, since we are surrounded by so great a cloud of witnesses, let us also lay aside every weight and the sin that clings so closely and let us run with perseverance the race that is set before us, looking to Jesus the pioneer and perfecter of our faith, who for the sake of the joy that was set before him endured the cross, disregarding its shame..." The same greek word is used here as in Acts 1:8 - witnesses. They testified; they witnessed to God's love and healing grace; they testified to the Christ at work in their lives. They testified to the love of Christ touching their hearts and souls, transforming their lives in radical ways of love and justice!

So we'll testify too. We'll tell the world about God's grace by reaching out to those in our community in need - because that's what Jesus did. We'll tell the world about God's grace by feeding those in our community who are hungry - because that's what Jesus did. We'll show love to children - because that's what Jesus did. We'll stand by those who are today's lepers - because that's what Jesus did!

We'll be witnesses to God's ongoing creation - because that's what Jesus did - and what he calls us to do.

We won't be the rulers, we won't hold power over anyone else, we won't hoard all our wealth - Jesus didn't ask us to do any of that. Jesus said, "you will be my witnesses in Jerusalem, in all Judea and Samaria, and to the ends of the earth."

So - the answer to our question - where do we go from here? - is clear. Our stories are now intertwined with God's story, so we'll link our arms together, face the path ahead, and, like Dorothy, the Tin Man, the Scarecrow, and that Cowardly Lion, we'll skip down the road, strengthened by the power of the

Holy Spirit witnessing to God's love, compassion and grace in Jesus the Christ!

May it be so always. Amen.

Don't They Know Who I Am?!
Luke 17:5-10

5 The apostles said to the Lord, "Increase our faith!" 6 The Lord replied, "If you had faith the size of a mustard seed, you could say to this mulberry tree, 'Be uprooted and planted in the sea,' and it would obey you.

7 "Who among you would say to your slave who has just come in from plowing or tending sheep in the field, 'Come here at once and take your place at the table'? 8 Would you not rather say to him, 'Prepare supper for me, put on your apron and serve me while I eat and drink; later you may eat and drink'? 9 Do you thank the slave for doing what was commanded? 10 So you also, when you have done all that you were ordered to do, say, 'We are worthless slaves; we have done only what we ought to have done!'"

We start today a long series of lectionary texts from the gospel attributed to Luke. Sadly, because I used the last four weeks to help us get to know each other better, our text today just sort of plunks us down in the middle of a long section in Luke about the journey of Jesus and the disciples from Galilee to Jerusalem. If we'd been in the lectionary all along, you'd've already read much of this section which goes from Luke 9:51 to 19:27. So here's your homework - before next Sunday, read from Luke 9:51 up through our Scripture for next week. Well shucks, while you're at it, you might as well read all of Luke up to where we'll be. Or read all of it if you're on a roll!

Next week, I'll take some time to give you a broad overview of Luke-Acts and how we might apply these texts to our church today in this place. You know, the ironic thing about this background material is that it's coming from a former Pastor of First Christian Church - Rev. Ron Allen! That's right, in the commentary we used at Seminary, he's the author of the chapters on Luke-Acts. Anyway, I'll make time next week to give you some of that information.

For today, we're just gonna dive into the deep end!

And it's really deep for the disciples, isn't it?! Asking for more faith doesn't seem like such a terrible request, does it? That's what starts this - you see, right before today's text, Jesus has told the disciples that they need to be prepared to correct people when they need it - and to forgive them when they ask - even if it's 7 times a day. "you must forgive," Jesus says.

Seems kind of sensible to ask for more faith to be doing all this forgiving, doesn't it? So why does Jesus put the apostles down with the mustard seed crack? And then why does he tell this odd story about slaves? And what does this have to do with the kingdom of God? Well, I think it has everything to do with it - it has everything to do with our human nature and how the kingdom turns that upside down. Make no mistake - this is difficult to wrap your head around - it flies in the face of what we might call common sense. Indeed, it is the apostles' quote 'common sense' unquote, that Jesus takes advantage of to make this teaching.

He takes their expectations and flips them around. Just when they think they're 'somebody', the rug gets yanked out - and they're nobody. Can't you just see the apostles fuming and thinking, 'But we're the top dogs around here - doesn't he know who we are?"

Doesn't it confuse you when you don't get the recognition you think you deserve? When you get slighted, doesn't it make you say to yourself, "Don't they know who I am?!!"

[pause]

Yeah, it makes me feel that way, too. And I'll tell you, I had no trouble thinking of examples of folks who've thought they were the top dog only to find others didn't think of them as highly as they did! Why else do celebrities get in so much trouble? Look at Brittney Spears and Lindsay Lohan's troubles, or Martha Stewart's, for that matter - Why did they think they could get away with what they did? Why did they say, in effect, "Don't you know who I am?!!" Ah well - those examples are too easy. I'll give you a not so public one. Men - have you ever felt hassled and put upon when your spouse has interrupted you to do some chore you've put off. Umm, hmmm... "Doesn't she know who I am?!" And you know it works both ways, women! You see? We all want to be the boss, we want to be in charge, we want to be the master.

And Jesus knows this! - that's why he puts us in the place of the master in this teaching - with his questions of "Who among you"... and "would you not rather say..." we immediately go there, we immediately grasp what he's saying about the role of the master, shucks, that's just how we'd like to treat people, so it's easy to understand this story from the point of view of the master. Don't they know who we are?!

I had a wonderful - well, maybe embarrassing is the better modifier - experience last week that really brought this home. I drove over to Nebraska City to attend the funeral services for Dud Fossberg, Brad Fossberg's father. I wasn't sure where the church was - and when I got to Nebraska City, the directions I had were wrong and I had to call Jane to get that straightened out. I finally found the church - and it was busy! All of the parking close to the church was taken so I had to find a place on the street several blocks away. As I found a spot, two other people got out of their car in the adjacent slot, leaving their doors open so I couldn't pull in until they were done. Don't they know who I am?!! I couldn't believe they were being so rude in blocking "my" space! Didn't they know I was Brad's Pastor and that I needed to get there?

Well, of course they didn't. But that didn't stop *me* from being willing to jump into the master role! I do have to say on my behalf, though, that I did recognize what a great example it was gonna make for today's sermon! And I think I've made my point. It's just easy for us to jump into master-type rolls, either out of a sense of false pride or egotistical self-centeredness, or simple self-righteousness about how we deserve to be treated, never worrying about how we're treating others as a result. For you see, the end of this teaching flips these rolls, it puts *us* in the slave place, the subservient place. I like the J. B. Phillips translation: "It is the same with yourselves - <u>when</u> you have done everything that you are told to do, you can say, "We are not much good as servants; we have only done what we ought to do."

But I don't know - do you think that could ever actually happen? Would the world be a better place if we served each other rather than looking to be served? Should we serve each other - just because we ought to? I wonder - you know, it reminds of someone I knew a long time ago. As I recall it....

A beautiful day can be made pretty miserable by getting a flat tire. Sometimes you can tell your tire is flat by the noise it makes and sometimes by the way the car starts wobbling. You know it's really flat when you get both symptoms. I did manage to get to the side of the road safely though.

It was a fall day, one with the sunlight streaming through the dry colored leaves making the dust in the air sparkle. I was on my way to a meeting in the little town of Spencerville. You've probably been there; it's that little town on the way from here to there. I was coming as a consultant for the town as they were considering a new subdivision and wanted some outside thought on the best mix of commercial/residential use. However, it looked like I was going to be late. I don't like flats and I don't like being late so my good nature was rapidly leaving in spite of the charming day and weather.

I was on the edge of town; there was the steeple of the Methodist church not too far in the distance and a few hundred yards ahead I could see an old, worn sign: Red's Auto Service. Maybe they could fix my tire if I took it off and rolled it down there. I opened the trunk and sighed. Of course the trunk was nearly full and the spare and the tire iron were at the bottom. Muttering to myself, I started yanking stuff around and weighing my options whether I should just take the flat off and run it down to Red's or go ahead and put on the spare all the while realizing I'd be late either way.

"Excuse me - can I help you?" came a voice at my side.

I straightened up defensively, who would be out here mid-morning with nothing better to do than accost stranded motorists, "Maybe. Who are you? Does Red's fix tires?" I asked.

"I'm sorry, my name's Tommy. You look like you could use a hand and I've got a couple hands…," he offered. "Yes, Red fixes tires so they stay fixed!"

At that, Tommy, stopped and smiled. It was a smile with no guile in it, no hint of avarice; it was the smile of someone who genuinely wanted to help and I couldn't help but smile back with a feeling of hope and relief!

"Well… I am close to being late for my meeting," I mentioned trying to gauge the time and the distance to Red's Auto Service. I weighed the cost of a lost spare tire verses the potential income from this contract and decided to trust Tommy, the fellow with the trusting smile! "You're sure it's not too much trouble? I wouldn't want to put you out or make you late for something too…"

"No, not at all! I'm going right by Red's anyhow and today's too nice to waste it on hurrying'" He helped set some of the clutter aside as I pulled out the tire from the bottom of the trunk and then we loaded everything back in, shut the trunk and I got my briefcase and locked the car.

"By the way, Tommy, my name's Scott - Scott Taylor. I can't tell you how much I appreciate your help." I reached for my wallet to give him some money to cover the repairs and pay him a little something but he waved me off, saying, "No need for that - you can pay Red for the tire and, like I said, I'm goin' that way anyhow!"

"Well, how can I find you? What's your phone number?" I asked.

"Oh you can always reach me at the Café, the Buttermilk Café down on the square. Just tell Elvira - she's the owner, and she'll make sure I get it. Now you better get goin' to your meeting…" he smiled encouragingly.

I knew I had to hurry but I just had to ask, "Why are you doing this?" Tommy replied, "'cause it needs doin'!" as he started rolling my tire down the side of the road!

A quick glance at my watch showed I needed to get a move on too; there was no time to ponder Tommy or his kind offer. Frankly, I have to admit, I dropped him from my thoughts as I hurried to the City Hall for my meeting. I was going to make it just a few minutes after the appointed time and the flat tire was as good an excuse as any for my tardiness!

Thankfully, the charming day and fair weather held and my meeting was concluded successfully. With a happy smile, I walked out of City Hall and saw the round sign of The Buttermilk Café - seemed like a good omen for a piece of celebratory pie and a cup of coffee! The red and white checkered tablecloths brought back memories of my college days making me feel welcomed in spite of it being the first time I'd ever been there. My luck was holding out as I could see Tommy sitting at the counter and there was a stool next to him free.

"Tommy! Just the person I need to see… mind if I sit here?"

"No, Scott - sure, have a seat. Elvira? Come say 'hello' to Scott - I told you about his tire earlier…" he added.

Elvira, looking every bit of the matron of the Café, came over wiping her hands on her apron. "Hi there, Scott - it's a pleasure to meet you - what can I get for you?"

"I'll have a piece of that peach pie and a cup of coffee and whatever Tommy'd like," I said.

"Coming right up!" was her reply. She glanced at Tommy and he smiled; I smiled and she smiled and everything seemed about as Mayberry as Andy Griffin!

"Everyone's sure friendly here, Tommy. I can't thank you enough for your help this morning. It looks like I'll be seeing you more often - I got the contract I was here to discuss." Tommy's eyes lifted and he shook my hand, "That's terrific!" he added.

"How can I repay you?" I asked sincerely.

"By passing me the creamer!" he grinned in reply as Elvira put my pie down. "You don't owe me anything, I was just doin' what I ought to," he mentioned. "You know how the dishes don't care who cleans them or how the trash doesn't care who takes it out? Well, your tire didn't care who rolled it down to Red's one bit! It just needed doin'" and he smiled. Again.

"You see, Scott, it's always a joy when you get to do what you ought to do - thank you for the chance!"

With that, Tommy sipped the last slurp in his cup, picked up his paper napkin and saucer and deposited them in the tub at the bussing station and waved a hand, "See ya around!"

I learned a simple lesson from Tommy that's served me well ever since. Be the change you want to see. Tommy didn't 'change' Spencerville - *he* was changed and, as a result, his whole world changed. Instead of living in a world where he *had* to do things, he lived in a world where he did things simply because he was supposed to! And so did those around him. I guess it worked on me too - I still clean up my dishes down at the Café - just doing what I ought to do!

That's the good news down in Spencerville. Amen!

God, Thank You, But...
Luke 18:9-14

9 He also told this parable to some who trusted in themselves that they were righteous and regarded others with contempt: 10 "Two men went up to the temple to pray, one a Pharisee and the other a tax collector. 11 The Pharisee, standing by himself, was praying thus, 'God, I thank you that I am not like other people: thieves, rogues, adulterers, or even like this tax collector. 12 I fast twice a week; I give a tenth of all my income.' 13 But the tax collector, standing far off, would not even look up to heaven, but was beating his breast and saying, 'God, be merciful to me, a sinner!' 14 I tell you, this man went down to his home justified rather than the other; for all who exalt themselves will be humbled, but all who humble themselves will be exalted."

Well, here's another one of those pesky, familiar parables we've all heard umpteen times before! And the author of Luke has given us a pretty straightforward answer or conclusion to it all: "for all who exalt themselves will be humbled, but all who humble themselves will be exalted."

Okay. I guess we can all go home now! Give me a break, Luke - is it really that simple? I don't know; that just feels too easy and - well - watered down. We've got so many ways of saying this, "Don't toot your own horn" and "Be careful who you judge lest you be judged" and things like that. Platitudes that go in one ear and out the other.

 [*pause*]

And what's so wrong about what the Pharisee is saying? As I sit with this text, my thoughts go to the Pharisee - and I agree with him! I'm glad I'm not a thief or a rogue! I'm truly glad I haven't ever robbed a bank. By the way, did you know that that's one of the least successful crimes you can do? Bank robbers almost always get caught. Just a word of caution...

And it's not just really obvious bad guys like that that I'm glad I'm not like. Have you driven way east on, say, 16th street? Eventually, you run into the railroad tracks. If you follow the underpass, on the other side, is a trailer park - Pioneer Park I think it's called. I got lost trying to find an address and I ended up driving through there. It's quite an eclectic collection! And I even have some sympathy for folks who live in trailer parks because I lived in a trailer park once myself. I'm glad I don't live in one now. [*pause*] That's terrible, isn't it? And I apologize to anyone here who lives in a trailer park! There's nothing wrong with trailer parks! But there it is, why would you believe me now after I've just said I'm glad I don't live in one anymore? What we say matters.

Now Tax Collectors - don't get me started! Actually, we need a different image here to be faithful to the context in Luke's time. The Jews were an occupied people - they lived under Roman rule - the "tax collector" was a Jew who worked for the Romans collecting the Roman tax and maybe lining their own pockets while they were at it! Many were extortionists, basically. So they were easy to look down upon. Nowadays, we've got so many folks we find easy to put down, don't we? Illegal aliens, drug dealers, government informants, etc., etc. I mean, let's face it, I'm really glad I don't do drugs...anymore and I'm glad I never cheated on my taxes...and got caught and... I suppose I'll just stop here!

You see? I end up focused on the Pharisee in this story - he makes sense! Oh, I don't want to be judgmental of people but haven't you felt like the Pharisee at least sometimes? Saying, "Thank you, God, but I'm sure glad I'm normal and not like those other people!" In fact, that's the problem with most of these folks on the Pharisee's list, isn't it? They're not normal - like us. Some singer/songwriter friends of mine, Rich and Jacqui, have a great song that sums this up - let's listen to a little of it:

> 'He was a cuff link, cut throat, duck top boyish man,
> hardnosed, Dow Jones, CEO, a snake in the grass,
> She was a high class, high toned, bleached blond socialite,
> lipo sucked, tummy tucked, stuck up - and she was his wife.
> He's mixing models in L.A., she rolls his Rolls into a lake,
> When she gets 30 million, lawyers take a holiday,
> They were made for love! Two hands, one whole.
> What heaven has brought upon us,
> let no one touch with a ten-foot pole!
> They're not normal like us!
> They're nothing like none of our friends,
> I know we may not be perfect;
> thank God we're nothing like them..."[1]

See? That's all the Pharisee is saying, "they're not normal - like us."

   [*pause*]

Of course, we hardly ever think or say stuff like this in such harsh language. We've got nice, genteel ways to say it. There's always the ubiquitous 'but'. We've all heard people say things like:

"I don't like to gossip, but..." and,

"That looks great, but..." and what about,

"I don't mean to butt in, but...!"

That 'but' let's us make the comparison, let's us make the judgment, let's us 'help' someone do better. That 'but' makes a dividing line between 'us' and 'them'. And that can lead to:

"Everyone's welcome here, but..." or,

"God loves everyone, but..."

Yeah, but. But God, if you'd just do things *this* way, *they'd* be better. I wonder. If God actually did things *this* way, would *we* be better? But remember... they're not normal - like us.

[*pause*]

Then there's my all-time favorite euphemism for that 'but', it's the phrase, 'bless her heart'. Yes! You know that one too?! You can say the most awful things about anyone if you just wrap it up with, "bless her heart!" Things like,

"She has the decorating taste of a blind person on prozac - bless her heart!" or,

"He's so pigheaded, he'd let his house burn down rather than ask for help, bless his heart!"

Do you see? They're not normal - like us. Thank you, God, but... They're so - whatever, bless their hearts!

'Us' verses 'them' - that's all this is. And that'd be another simple conclusion to this text but it's not that simple. The Pharisee isn't out at Walmart, he's in the Temple - the holy place, sacred ground. And he's not talking to anyone, he's 'standing by himself' the parable says. 'Praying' the parable says. And it's a wonder he even notices the tax collector. The parable says the tax collector was 'standing far off'. So if the Pharisee is praying, even praying for things I think I'd pray for too, how does he even notice the tax collector? How can he be paying attention to God if he's gawking all around the Temple? And then saying stuff like he's something special - "I fast twice a week; I give a tenth of all my income" as though that was a big deal. Yeah, right, he's 'praying', *bless his heart*!

On the other hand, there's this tax collector. He's not looking around; he's not even looking up to heaven. And he's not saying 'thank you' to God or anything.

In fact, he's not comparing himself or his actions with anyone. He says, with no reference to anyone else, "God, be merciful to me, a sinner!" No 'buts', no 'thank God, we're nothing like them!' Nothing to distract him from God; nothing to come between him and God.

You see, that's what I wonder about. Do I, like the Pharisee, get so caught up in my own sense of righteousness that I take my eye and heart off God and end up playing God and separating my world into 'us' - 'them'? I wonder, just how distracting could this be?

> [*move away from the pulpit*]

I wear this robe and stole - like a Pharisee - someone respected for religious knowledge and practice. I lead us in prayer - just like I did this morning. But what if I didn't do the normal thing? What if I didn't wear this robe or stole? [*take the robe and stole off*] What if I didn't have any shoes on? [*slip off shoes*] What if I was sipping from a bottle of water as I prayed? "God, be merciful to me, a sinner!" [*take water bottle - take a sip and set it on the communion table*] Would it distract you? Would I be less than normal? Would you be thinking, 'He's a pretty good minister, *bless his heart*...'?

> [*put shoes, robe, etc. back on - take water off table*]

Or would you be listening with God and praying to God saying, "God, be merciful to me, a sinner!" no matter whether I was a Pharisee or a tax collector or was dressed like a bum or not? Would you see 'us' verses 'them' or only 'us'? Who's praying to God - and who's praying to himself?

Makes you wonder, doesn't it?

May it be so always. Amen.

---

[1] *Waltz of the Wallflowers (A Dysfunctional Duet)*, Small Potatoes, Wind River Publishing, 2000.

A Never Ending Buffet
John 4:5-42

5 So he came to a Samaritan city called Sychar, near the plot of ground that Jacob had given to his son Joseph. 6 Jacob's well was there, and Jesus, tired out by his journey, was sitting by the well. It was about noon.

7 A Samaritan woman came to draw water, and Jesus said to her, "Give me a drink." 8 (His disciples had gone to the city to buy food.) 9 The Samaritan woman said to him, "How is it that you, a Jew, ask a drink of me, a woman of Samaria?" (Jews do not share things in common with Samaritans.) 10 Jesus answered her, "If you knew the gift of God, and who it is that is saying to you, 'Give me a drink,' you would have asked him, and he would have given you living water." 11 The woman said to him, "Sir, you have no bucket, and the well is deep. Where do you get that living water? 12 Are you greater than our ancestor Jacob, who gave us the well, and with his sons and his flocks drank from it?" 13 Jesus said to her, "Everyone who drinks of this water will be thirsty again, 14 but those who drink of the water that I will give them will never be thirsty. The water that I will give will become in them a spring of water gushing up to eternal life." 15 The woman said to him, "Sir, give me this water, so that I may never be thirsty or have to keep coming here to draw water."

16 Jesus said to her, "Go, call your husband, and come back." 17 The woman answered him, "I have no husband." Jesus said to her, "You are right in saying, 'I have no husband'; 18 for you have had five husbands, and the one you have now is not your husband. What you have said is true!" 19 The woman said to him, "Sir, I see that you are a prophet. 20 Our ancestors worshiped on this mountain, but you say that the place where people must worship is in Jerusalem." 21 Jesus said to her, "Woman, believe me, the hour is coming when you will worship the Father neither on this mountain nor in Jerusalem. 22 You worship what you do not know; we worship what we know, for salvation is from the Jews. 23 But the hour is coming, and is now here, when the true worshipers will worship the Father in spirit and truth, for the Father seeks such as these to worship him. 24 God is spirit, and those who worship him must worship in spirit and truth." 25 The woman said to him, "I know that Messiah is coming" (who is called Christ). "When he comes, he will proclaim all things to us." 26 Jesus said to her, "I am he, the one who is speaking to you."

27 Just then his disciples came. They were astonished that he was speaking with a woman, but no one said, "What do you want?" or, "Why are you speaking with her?" 28 Then the woman left her water jar and went back to the city. She said to the people, 29 "Come and see a man who told me everything I have ever done! He cannot be the Messiah, can he?" 30 They left the city and were on their way to him.

31 Meanwhile the disciples were urging him, "Rabbi, eat something." 32 But he said to them, "I have food to eat that you do not know about." 33 So the disciples said to one another, "Surely no one has brought him something to eat?" 34 Jesus said to them, "My food is to do the will of him who sent me and to complete his work. 35 Do you not say, 'Four months more, then comes the harvest'? But I tell you, look around you, and see how the fields are ripe for harvesting. 36 The reaper is already receiving wages and is gathering fruit for eternal life, so that sower and reaper may rejoice together. 37 For here the saying holds true, 'One sows and another reaps.' 38 I sent you to reap that for which you did not labor. Others have labored, and you have entered into their labor."

39 Many Samaritans from that city believed in him because of the woman's testimony, "He told me everything I have ever done." 40 So when the Samaritans came to him, they asked him to stay with them; and he stayed there two days. 41 And many more believed because of his word. 42 They said to the woman, "It is no longer because of what you said that we believe, for we have heard for ourselves, and we know that this is truly the Savior of the world."

I have to admit, I do enjoy a good buffet! I told you a few weeks ago how my friend and I used to go to Golden Corral - 'grazing at the Corral' we used to say. But even there, we'd have to stop - eventually. There are only so many trips to the salad and dessert bar you can make, you know? It sure was fun while it lasted. But in the end, we'd get full and have to go try to work for the rest of the afternoon, slowed down by full bellies and stuffed, sleepy heads. And then wouldn't you know it? The very next day we'd be hungry and thirsty again.

So one of the first things that caught my attention in reading our text for today is the allure of 'living water' - "those who drink of the water that I will give them will never be thirsty," Jesus says. And he talks about "food to eat that you do not know about." Is this some sort of 'heavenly buffet' where we can partake and never thirst or hunger again? In a way, yes. Of course, Jesus isn't talking about food and drink, no he's talking about a deeper need for spiritual sustenance, the stuff of life that gives us meaning and purpose and eternal life. Man, that sounds intriguing, doesn't it? I mean, wouldn't you want that? Wouldn't you want to go see what was going on if someone told you about that? Wouldn't you take time out of your busy week to come and see?

Or would it depend on who told you? I don't know - there's some people, if they told me something like that, I'm thinking I'd take it with a grain of salt - I'd probably smile and nod encouragingly as they told me but all the while I'm saying in the back of my mind, "they haven't got a clue - *bless their heart!*"

[*pause*]

Which gets me to something that's always bugged me about this text. Why does Jesus pick a woman to talk with to spread the news? And a Samaritan woman at that! I mean, he's a prophet, isn't he? The woman said so and told everyone, "Come and see a man who told me everything I have ever done!" so he's got to be insightful, wouldn't you think?

So why's he so bad at human resources - at personnel? Come on, in biblical times, women stayed in their place - it's even odd that she'll speak to Jesus at the well. The disciples know this, "They were astonished that he was speaking with a woman," the text says. And the text also makes it clear that, well, let's just say that Samaritans and Jews may have been relatives and neighbors but they didn't see eye to eye if you know what I mean! Nosiree, there were no 'get to know your neighbor' block parties back then!

So why in the world does Jesus pick - her - to spread the news? And make no mistake, in this story, she's important. In the whole story, the only people who speak are Jesus, the disciples, and this - woman. And the disciples only get two short lines to fill out the plot; they're certainly not the main characters. No, for some reason, Jesus picked this woman, this foreigner, this outsider, this damaged goods woman, married five times and now with a partner she's not even married to! What was he thinking?

Or is this just some bad judgement character trait he got from his dad?

Yeah - I said it - I mean, let's face - God picks oddballs too! Yeah - that's right - God's not very good at personnel management, if you ask me. Look at the record - he picked Abraham and Sarah to found a great nation - when they didn't have a home and were way too old to have kids! And let's not even talk about some of the things Abraham did when he was younger. Then he picks Jacob, a thief who tricked his own brother out of the birthright, and then what about Moses? He stuttered and whined and finally God had to just flat put God's foot down to make him go to Egypt. And then he picked David, the littlest one in that family and an adulterer eventually. And on and on.

Is this any way to run creation?

So, I guess Jesus comes by his questionable personnel judgement skills naturally. So it's no wonder he picks fishermen and women and tax collectors and lepers and - Samaritans. What can you expect? Like father, like son, I guess. Can you imagine any self-respecting business picking some unqualified unknown outsider to run their PR campaign to get their message out there?

Sheesh! The way Jesus picks people, he just might pick one of us to spread the news! Can you imagine that? You - or you - or you - going out to tell your neighbors about this amazing buffet Jesus has to offer. Or would you listen to this cockamamy tale and then just stay home, thinking, "bless his heart..."? Just stay home, a sort of 'couch-potato christian', snacking all the time because you know we're always a little hungry and thirsty! We don't get 'a never-ending buffet' that way. No, it's this Samaritan woman, this outsider, who gets it even as she sasses Jesus and questions herself. She believed and not just as a static sort of thing, a belief. No, she 'believed' - the verb, to believe - it took some action on her part. Well - don't take my word for it, here, listen to her brother...

My sister, Amerah, came home, excited, shouting, Eli! Eli! I'm her brother and the eldest son. I thought she was maybe confused or dazed by the midday heat but she really believed what she'd seen and heard and couldn't keep it to herself. She'd met this prophet, she said, down at the well - Jacob's well. She said his name was Jesus and he was a Jew from Galilee. I know! It's hard to believe, Jesus' message coming to us. He's a Jew - would it be possible salvation could come to Samaritans too?

My sister was persistent though, she said he told her everything about her life. She seemed to *have* to tell us about this Jesus - her believing made her do it, and it was infectious - made us want to go hear too! She talked about something called 'living water' and worshipping in spirit and truth. I found it hard to understand - but what if...?

What if I truly believe? Then I've got to go tell someone else, I've got to change - it doesn't happen, this living water, if I just stay home! Amerah wouldn't stop telling us, she wouldn't stop asking us if he's the messiah so we had to go check it out and then we believed too. Jesus stayed with us for several days and many more heard for themselves - all because my sister, Amerah, 'believed' to us!

Eli and Amerah - characters that could be in our story today. Remember the greek verb for 'to believe'? *pisteuo*? I mentioned it last week. It's used in John over 90 times. You see? You've got to do something with it. The Samaritan woman does something - she believes. She believes all the way into town, she believes to her neighbors, she believes to her family, and they begin believing to their friends and family too.

"For God so loved the world that he gave his only son, so that everyone who has faith in him, who believes in him, may not perish but have eternal life." Remember? This isn't a nice platitude to make us feel good as we sit back relaxing. No, this is a call to action. No couch potato Christians for John, nosiree, you've got to go 'believe', not just have 'a belief'. We've got to go act on it, we've got to go 'believe' it in our own lives; we've got to go 'believe' it to others. And remember, this is Jesus' never-ending buffet, which is apparently being offered to outcasts, and Samaritans and everyone - not just to those who think and act like we do.

Jesus calls us to a buffet alright - one overflowing with living water and spirit - he offered it to a Samaritan woman. Jesus - God - the worst personnel directors ever - or maybe the wisest - deepest - and most loving. "So that everyone who believes" - including us - can 'believe' it all over the world!

That is good news, indeed! Amen.

It's Just A Baby Boy
Matthew 2:13-23

13 Now after they had left, an angel of the Lord appeared to Joseph in a dream and said, "Get up, take the child and his mother, and flee to Egypt, and remain there until I tell you; for Herod is about to search for the child, to destroy him." 14 Then Joseph got up, took the child and his mother by night, and went to Egypt, 15 and remained there until the death of Herod. This was to fulfill what had been spoken by the Lord through the prophet, "Out of Egypt I have called my son."

16 When Herod saw that he had been tricked by the wise men, he was infuriated, and he sent and killed all the children in and around Bethlehem who were two years old or under, according to the time that he had learned from the wise men. 17 Then was fulfilled what had been spoken through the prophet Jeremiah:

18 "A voice was heard in Ramah, wailing and loud lamentation, Rachel weeping for her children; she refused to be consoled, because they are no more."

19 When Herod died, an angel of the Lord suddenly appeared in a dream to Joseph in Egypt and said, 20 "Get up, take the child and his mother, and go to the land of Israel, for those who were seeking the child's life are dead." 21 Then Joseph got up, took the child and his mother, and went to the land of Israel. 22 But when he heard that Archelaus was ruling over Judea in place of his father Herod, he was afraid to go there. And after being warned in a dream, he went away to the district of Galilee. 23 There he made his home in a town called Nazareth, so that what had been spoken through the prophets might be fulfilled, "He will be called a Nazorean."

Boy, here's a story full of intrigue and sorrow and harrowing escapes! Exciting stuff - just the sort of stuff you might see on the news today. In fact, as much as I've tried over the past week to find some way to spin this, the eerie parallels to our world wouldn't let me go. This is a story about terrorism, isn't it?!

You might need some more background information though to really see the connection. Judah was a land filled with turmoil back then. First, there was the Maccabean war that led to the Hasmodian kings who were no fun - they introduced Greek cults into the Temple offending many Jews. Then, in 63 BCE, the Roman General, Pompey, conquered Palestine making it a province of the Roman empire. While Roman rule had beneficial effects, there were repeated calls to revolt against the unpopular Imperial rule. Of course, these were brutally squashed; on one occasion, the Romans crucified as many as 2000 rebels outside Jerusalem.

So Herod, the Roman protege` who ruled from 37 to 4 BCE, knew something about terrorists and revolution. He probably had a network of informants and spies who provided intelligence. And how can you blame Herod? He was facing risks - risks to the freedom and safety of his country. Of course he wanted to protect himself and his people. So he got some intelligence - good intelligence - that there was a possible leader coming, a leader who would crush Herod and the Empire - like the revolts back in the Maccabean days.

So Herod reacts. He ponders, he brings in suspects and interviews them, trying to get information so he can protect the country and Empire from terror and revolt. His advisors say there's a clear threat, he should take preemptive measures. They've got to go with the information they've got and not wait, not look for other solutions. So Herod does what he has to do and kills all the boy children he can get his hands on. But you see, he's not really killing children, he's trying to protect and alleviate what he sees as a clear threat and danger. The fact that they're children and civilians is overshadowed by the perceived threat.

But you know some of them got away! He couldn't move that fast - the news had to spread and I'm guessing Mary and Joseph weren't the only ones running for their lives. I'll bet there were real refugee problems and tragedies in and around Palestine back then.

You see? This sort of reaction rather than response gets us into trouble all the time. And what's this threat Herod has to react to so strongly? It's just a baby. Just a baby boy. But, in the end, it doesn't matter whether it's Herod's soldiers or one of our smart bombs or a suicide bomber outside of Islamabad that does the killing - in the end, the children are dead and Rachel is weeping for her children; she refuses to be consoled, because they are no more.

> [*pause*]

Well - enough about reaction verses response, that's not what this story's about in the end anyway, it's really about angels and God and getting up and going! Of course, it's also a very well-crafted story - did you notice the great storytelling effects? You can tell this was a story people listened to rather than read. Well, of course, *all* the scriptures were heard rather than read - that's why listening to them is so important, that's why I say, "People of God - *Hear* these words" as I read the scripture. But this one's got great earmarks of storytelling, listen to it this way:

This is a story about how the baby Jesus almost got killed. After he'd been born, as his mom and dad were deciding when to go home, an angel appeared to his dad, Joseph, in a dream and said, "Get up, take the child and his mother, and flee to Egypt, and remain there until I tell you; Herod is about to search for your son, to kill him!" So Joseph got up, and he and Mary and baby Jesus fled that very night and went to Egypt. And there they stayed until Herod died. And die he did in the course of his days.

Right after Herod died, again an angel suddenly appeared in a dream to Joseph way far away in Egypt and said, "Get up, take Jesus and Mary, and go to the land of Israel, for those who were seeking the child's life are dead." So Joseph got up, and he and Mary and Jesus went to the land of Israel. But when he heard that Archelaus was ruling over Judea in place of his father Herod, he was afraid to go there! But after being warned yet again in a dream, they went to Galilee and settled in the little village of Nazareth. And 'til this very day, that's why we know Jesus as a Nazorean.

Three times Joseph gets warned in a dream. Three times an angel brings him a message. And three times, Joseph 'gets up' and does what the angel told him to do. "Three times" is a big deal in storytelling - there's something about mentioning a thing three times that makes it stick, that makes it memorable.

[pause]

You know, if an angel appears to me in a dream - even once - I'm thinking I'm gonna remember it! Have you ever had an angel appear to you in a dream and say, "Get up!"? Have you ever had an angel appear and say anything? Anything at all? If you have, I'd love to hear from you; I'd love to sit and listen to your story, I really would.

Me? No, I've never had an angel appear to me in a dream, at least never in a dream I remember. I wonder... if an angel visits you in your dreams and you don't wake up and remember it, do you still get to say you did? And if I can't recall an angel's visit, does that mean God's not trying to talk to me? Or maybe, just maybe - God's simply had a lot more practice by now and no longer needs to get our attention by appearing in our dreams?

Think about it. Way back in the mythological beginning, God speaks directly to Adam and Eve and Cain and Noah. But by the time we get to Moses, God's just speaking to Moses and then only when Moses is away from the people. And this goes on too. The prophets begin hearing God in visions, in dreams - God speaks less and less directly. By the time we get to the New Testament, there's only a few times when God speaks directly - Jesus'

Transfiguration being the main place. Now, it's the angels in dreams and visions. Then at Pentecost, it's tongues of flame from the Holy Spirit. And when you get to Paul and even to the Epistles, it's through regular human beings that God speaks.

For make no mistake - God is still speaking - just maybe not in quite so spectacular a fashion as angels in dreams. And I think God is still saying "Get up!" and do whatever it is that we need to do. You noticed, didn't you, that that's the other half of the storytelling method. It isn't enough just to have an angel appear and say, "Get up!" No, the thing that wraps it all up is Joseph's response - he "gets up!" He goes to Egypt, he comes back to Israel, he settles in Nazareth. He doesn't just respond once; he responds each time the angel or God or whatever appears to him.

You know what I think? I think God's not so much interested in impressing us with flashy visits in dreams - I think God's much more interested in what we do with those visits. I think the visits wouldn't have made much difference if Joseph hadn't responded. It wouldn't be much of a story if it went like this:

This is a story about how the baby Jesus got killed. After he'd been born, as his mom and dad were deciding when to go home, an angel appeared to his dad, Joseph, in a dream and said, "Get up, take the child and his mother, and flee to Egypt, and remain there until I tell you; Herod is about to search for your son, to kill him!" But Joseph either didn't remember the dream or he simply said, 'nah, we're gonna stay here - Herod'll never find us." Wrong!

You see? It doesn't make nearly as good a story! In fact if Joseph hadn't "gotten up," we probably wouldn't even be talking about this story. But Joseph did. And Jesus lived to grow up. But, for now, he's just a baby - just a baby boy.

    [*pause*]

So how does God talk to us? How does God talk to you? Me, I think God's gotten pretty subtle. I've had a few experiences that I take as God talking directly to me and they've all included situations where other people have responded in ways that suggest God's activity. Or they've involved visions of sorts. I see things in new ways. Usually, it's 'me' I see in new ways and maybe that's not so far off from Joseph's experience.

Remember, Joseph, at least in Matthew's account, has an angel appear to him in a dream before Jesus is even born - and he stays with Mary as a result. So Joseph's only in the stable with Mary and the newborn baby because the angel told him to go. Maybe he sees himself as just continuing to be righteous. But something changes. Who knows? Maybe he really did have an amazing dream. But maybe he also saw himself holding the baby - *his* baby now - and he changed from Mary's husband to Jesus' dad. Maybe he saw himself in a whole new way, he saw what needed doing - and he got up and did it. He took Mary and Jesus and fled! What father - wanting to protect his family - wouldn't do that?

I had the rare privilege of spending some time with James Ellis and his son Parker when Parker was in the hospital recently. I saw a father who deeply loves his son and who would do anything he could to take care of all of his children and his family. God spoke to me that week through the Ellis family. God showed me what love can look like and I see myself differently as a result.

And recently, I saw a table, right out there in the Friendship room, covered with shoeboxes filled with gifts for children who probably weren't going to get much otherwise. And then I saw the faces of the people who delivered those shoeboxes and I saw how their lives were changed. Somehow, God spoke to them. I don't know if it was in a dream or not. But you know how I know God spoke to them? Because they 'got up'. Because they responded! I have no idea what they saw in their dreams - I have no more idea about that than whether Joseph saw anything in his dreams!

I know God's still speaking because I see people responding. I see people 'get up' and go do what needs doing. I see people 'get up' and build relationships. I see us 'get up' and be here each Sunday - smiling and happy to be here because God's touched us - somehow - someway.

Who knows whether it's angels in dreams or spirits or sheer mystery? Something calls to us, "Get up!" And we do. You know who I think it is that calls to us? I think it's that baby…it's just a little baby boy.

Amen.

My Child, My Beloved
Matthew 3: 13-17

13 Then Jesus came from Galilee to John at the Jordan, to be baptized by him. 14 John would have prevented him, saying, "I need to be baptized by you, and do you come to me?" 15 But Jesus answered him, "Let it be so now; for it is proper for us in this way to fulfill all righteousness." Then he consented. 16 And when Jesus had been baptized, just as he came up from the water, suddenly the heavens were opened to him and he saw the Spirit of God descending like a dove and alighting on him. 17 And a voice from heaven said, "This is my Son, the Beloved, with whom I am well pleased."

Do you believe God loves us? I think God does; I really do. And you know what else I think? I think this story is really about God's love for all of us but I'm getting a little bit ahead of myself. Let's take a closer look at all of this baptism stuff and how the different scriptures deal with it.

In order to do that, we're going to have to do some basic study work, some basic Bible study and understanding. Don't worry, there won't be a quiz and we will get back to the fun stuff about God loving us and all. But first, grab your Bible and turn to Mark 1:9-11. While you're finding that, a little background on the synoptic gospels, Matthew, Mark, and Luke. They weren't written at the same time nor in the same place so they've got obvious differences but there's lots of similarities too. In fact, scholars are sure that Mark was the first narrative gospel assembled - it was written not too long after Paul's letters, which are actually the earliest written documents we've got. Mark was written during the time of the destruction of the temple in 70 CE: it's terse and fast paced and scary and abrupt. Matthew and Luke, on the other hand, were written later and they each had their own audiences so the writers tailored their accounts for their time and audience, adding and editing as they felt the need.

But no matter how they did that, it's not hard to see that Matthew and Luke both had Mark available. So they just copied stuff from Mark's account in many cases. This story of Jesus' baptism is one of those that comes originally from Mark. Okay, you should have the text by now: [*read Mark 1:9-11*] See how much shorter and direct it is? Now turn to Luke 3:21-22. Or, take out your Gospel Parallels - or look at ours out in the Friendship Room sometime. Makes it really easy to see how the narratives line up. Okay, Luke: [*read Luke 3:21-22*] See how Luke is virtually the same as Mark? Matthew's the one who really edits a lot. In Mark and Luke, John the Baptist simply baptizes Jesus - there's no recognition of Jesus' special nature until *after* the baptism, only in Matthew's account does John recognize Jesus beforehand. And Matthew edits the ending too. In Mark and Luke, God speaks only to Jesus. In Matthew, God announces Jesus' status to everyone who's present.

But the thing that makes it a real parallel is God's response to Jesus' baptism: "You are my son, my beloved; with you I am well-pleased." Mmm Mmmm, just gives you a warm feeling all over, doesn't it, that feeling of being loved? [*take deep breath and smile; pause*]

You know, I can't help myself, my goofy mind just asks questions all the time. And as I sit thinking and savoring this story, I wonder - why'd Jesus do it? Why'd he decide to get baptized? Did his friends egg him on or was it his idea? What if his friends did put him up to it? What might that have been like?

I may just be guessing, but it could've been something like this.

Now Jesus grew up in the little town of Nazareth. He was a good kid and he had two best friends - Murray Goldblatt and Itzak Silverman, a couple of neighbors. Good Jewish kids, they all played together, they all went to school together and, they all got into trouble together! Jesus was the sharpest at studying the Torah; somehow, he just saw the big picture and could make sense of things that seemed to not be connected at all, at least it seemed like that to Itzak. Poor Itzak - studying with the Rabbi left his head spinning! He'd much rather be climbing one of the local olive trees or wrestling or organizing donkey races. Why, if there'd been a Jerusalem Temple Track and Field team, Itzak would've gotten a scholarship. Yeah, he was probably the one who spotted John way out in the wilderness first anyway, what with his cross country running.

Murray, on the other hand, was the true intellectual of the group. He'd been to Sephoris more than Itzak or even Jesus. Sephoris was that coast town not too far away from Nazareth that Herod had tried to turn into a Roman resort. He'd build great palaces and a modern waterfront and that had meant commerce and people from all over the world. Greek philosophy thrilled Murray - Plato, Socrates - he loved listening to the debates in Sephoris and would come back and tell Jesus and Itzak all about them. Heck, he and Jesus would argue sometimes and wrangle back and forth about the meaning of life and stuff like that. Eventually, Itzak would get hungry and whine, "Can't we go get a snack or something? Does your mom have any leftovers? What about a few dates? An olive or two? I'm starving here!"

So who's idea was it to go get baptized? There's no way to know - the gospels are silent about who's idea it was. Of course, Matthew adds the stuff about

John recognizing Jesus and Jesus saying, "Let it be so now; for it is proper for us in this way to fulfill all righteousness." Even today, this is still an important question - how do we decide to get baptized? And why? Shucks, I was baptized as an infant. To be honest, I really can't recall saying to my folks when I was 6 months old, "Mom, Dad - I know God loves me and I really want to follow Jesus and be baptized." No, I probably said something like [*baby talk*]

We Disciples are rightly proud of our restoration heritage; our founders looked to the early church as recorded in Acts and determined that baptism was something that only a believer could do. Look at Acts 2:37-41 sometime - that's believers baptism. So it makes a difference, this decision to be baptized. "Repent and be baptized every one of you in the name of Jesus Christ so that your sins may be forgiven;" Peter says in Acts. Right before our text for today, John the Baptist says in 3:2, "Repent, for the kingdom of heaven has come near. - in 3:11, "I baptize you with water for repentance..."

I don't think it was Itzak who suggested they go out to the Jordan river - oh, surely it was Itzak who said, "Yeah, I'll go - I can even show you guys the way out to John, I've been out that way running in the mornings." But his idea? I don't think so. It could've been Murray, he was serious about wanting to know God, he was surely aware of John. But I don't know - I can't see Murray thinking God had done anything special directly for or to him. He was too much caught up in the Platonic ideal of the Good and spirit versus material to respond to the weird idea that God loved him. Oh he knew God came into history, the great stories of the exodus from Egypt and the tales of King David and even the Prophets made it clear YHWH was a living God. But Murray was the legalistic one in their group and he was a good Jewish kid who followed the rules.

No, I'm guessing it was Jesus' idea. Jesus was the one who knew the Torah, who could argue with the Rabbis. He was the one who cut through the legalism of the law to see how love and compassion and charity ran through all of it. Oh, he wasn't the only one to see that, the great Jewish scholars of the time thought that interpretation of the Torah required looking at the texts through the lens of charity to others. But I'm guessing Jesus took that in and saw God's love as the over-arching theme of the scriptures.

I'll bet he argued with Murray about how God had to be love since they certainly didn't deserve God's concern, not with the things they'd done. Like the time they'd put a scorpion in Murray's sister's bed and she'd been so scared she wouldn't sleep in a bed for two months! Or when they'd been fooling around at the local well and had poked a few holes in the water skins of the Roman troops going through the town - they'd gotten the whole town in trouble with that trick! No, if God was for them and with them it had to be out of love.

Boy, I can understand that one - there's people who probably still don't want to have anything to do with me because of the inconsiderate, selfish things I did to them - People will give up on you - God never does.

Jesus recognized that - so did John, that's why he was baptizing. So my bet is this whole 'go get baptized' idea was Jesus's. But you know Murray and Itzak went along - those kids did everything together.

So there they are, John baptizes them and, you know, they really felt - something. They felt - loved, forgiven, somehow given new life. Last week, Linda Livingston felt that. Last week, we all felt a twinge of that, even if we were baptized as infants. That sense of being loved, just as we are, that sense of being forgiven for the mean-spirited ways we treat each other. I don't want to treat people that way. Jesus felt that too, for Jesus, in many ways, was no different than us. He was a human being, right down here with the rest of us, right down there with Murray and Itzak.

You know what I think? I think that's what baptism is about and that's why Jesus chose to be baptized. God's love for us is *because* God knows us, God isn't somewhere looking down, no, God is right there with *us*, holding *us* as we shiver and dip under the waters - loving *us*.

When Itzak popped back up, God was there, when Murray nearly fell back under because his foot slipped, God was there, and when Jesus pushed his hair back from his eyes, God was there. Maybe the writers only wrote down God's words for Jesus, but God says these words when *anyone* is baptized, "You are my child, my beloved, with whom I am well-pleased."

And that - is good news indeed! Amen.

A Pretty Fishy Story
Matthew 4:12-23

12 Now when Jesus heard that John had been arrested, he withdrew to Galilee. 13 He left Nazareth and made his home in Capernaum by the sea, in the territory of Zebulun and Naphtali, 14 so that what had been spoken through the prophet Isaiah might be fulfilled:

15 "Land of Zebulun, land of Naphtali, on the road by the sea, across the Jordan, Galilee of the Gentiles—16 the people who sat in darkness have seen a great light, and for those who sat in the region and shadow of death light has dawned."

17 From that time Jesus began to proclaim, "Repent, for the kingdom of heaven has come near." 18 As he walked by the Sea of Galilee, he saw two brothers, Simon, who is called Peter, and Andrew his brother, casting a net into the sea—for they were fishermen. 19 And he said to them, "Follow me, and I will make you fish for people." 20 Immediately they left their nets and followed him. 21 As he went from there, he saw two other brothers, James son of Zebedee and his brother John, in the boat with their father Zebedee, mending their nets, and he called them. 22 Immediately they left the boat and their father and followed him. 23 Jesus[c] went throughout Galilee, teaching in their synagogues and proclaiming the good news[d] of the kingdom and curing every disease and every sickness among the people.

My goodness, but this text is chocked full of stuff! Once again, the author of Matthew goes to the Hebrew scriptures to give credence to his story. His use of repetition is wonderful too. I've always loved the way he puts the very same words on Jesus' lips that John the Baptist spoke just a chapter earlier: "Repent, for the kingdom of heaven has come near." And then comes the part of this text that I loved - it's a fishing story!

Now, I'm no great shakes as a fisherman. When I was growing up, we used to take summer vacations at the beach and that time of one month of fishing in the surf or in the bay were the extent of my fishing experience. We mostly used squid for bait. [*slight pause*] I can't count the number of pieces of squid I threaded onto hooks fishing for blowfish and flounder and porgies. To be frank, that's why I can't eat calamari. I'm sorry, but I just can't eat bait!

[*pause*]

We never did much freshwater fishing; I don't know why. Oh, sure, we did some and I've caught some bluegills over the years - sunfish - we called 'em. But I never went trout fishing or bass fishing or even fishing for catfish. So I wouldn't say I'm a fisherman. But we've got some fishermen here for sure!

I know Kevin Crook's enjoyed some good fishing - I saw photographs when I visited he and Teri last week! And I know Volney Lofgreen loves to fish and I know Steve Millnitz even has his own special part of the Snake river up near Valentine where he loves to go. I know that Marcella's husband loved to fish too - what marvelous trophies are mounted on her living room wall. And I know there are others who love to fish too; I hope to come visit and see your photos and trophies sometime.

So fishing is something we know a little bit about, at least some of us. My friend, Tommy, was a fisherman, too. You remember Tommy, don't you? I met him in Spencerville, that little town on the way to wherever you're going. Tommy invited me to go fishing one spring weekend. There's a beautiful pond just south of town on Ted Baker's farm, shaded by cottonwood trees. As I said, it was early spring but the cottonwoods weren't snowing yet.

Once we got there, Tommy cast out his line and settled in - he didn't say a word and I didn't know whether to talk so I shut up too. It reminded me of something Volney told me once, "If you go sit out by a pond all afternoon, people will think you're eccentric, odd. But if you go sit out by a pond all afternoon - with a fishing pole in your hands - people will call you a sportsman!" Well, Tommy didn't much care what people called him but we had fishing poles in our hands this day!

Half an hour later, I asked, "I wonder how God fishes?"

Tommy smiled, reeled in his line and opened the small Styrofoam cooler that I thought had lunch. No, he had all sorts of bait in it! Worms, minnows, bacon, bread balls, gum drops, red bell pepper, tinsel as well as an assortment of flies and lures! He just smiles that smile that says, "It doesn't get any better than this," and pokes through the cooler. He tries a worm and pretty soon he caught a little bluegill. I swear, for the next hour, with each bait, he caught a different fish.

I caught a few but Tommy caught one of everything! It was almost like the fish wanted to get on Tommy's hook! I guess you could say that was the day that Tommy taught me how God fishes.

    [pause]

Jesus, in the gospel stories, is always cast as a carpenter but I think he was a fisherman too. And a pretty darn good one at that! How did he know what bait to use? Or was he the 'ultimate' bait himself? And just what constitutes 'good bait' when it comes to 'fishing for people'? Whatever Jesus had, it was good, wasn't it? The story tells us Jesus said, "Follow me, and I will make you fish for people. Immediately they left their nets and followed him." Immediately. That would be like casting your line in and bam, there's a strike! Whatever Jesus has, it's mighty good bait.

Or is Jesus himself - the bait? If he's going to make his disciples fish for people, does that mean they're now the bait? And if Jesus is still calling to us, "Follow me, and I will make you fish for people," does that mean we're - bait?

So I ask again - just what constitutes 'good bait' when you're fishing for people? And are we - 'good bait'? Just as I asked last week, what made you want to 'come... and see? And stay? What hooked you? And what can we do to become the best bait there is?! So I thought about it, and yeah, I think I know some of what it takes to be 'good bait'. Here's my top five 'good bait characteristics':

    1) Hospitality, strong community, good facilities

    2) Lots of different activities - not a 'one size fits all'

    3) We're authentic - we walk the walk not just talk the talk - compassionate

    4) Meaningful, engaging worship - strong prayer life

    5) Good stewards - good financial management - joyful givers, striving for stewardship as a spiritual discipline

I'm sure that we can find more 'good bait' characteristics, and that we can work on the ones I've already identified. Shucks, with Jesus as our fishing guide, we'll be reelin' 'em in immediately too! Why, with Jesus to help us, we'll be some of the best bait around - we might even have to change our name to the First Christian Church and Bait Shop!

And that is Good News, indeed. Amen.

Blazing Glory? Or Stewardship?
Matthew 17:1-9

17 Six days later, Jesus took with him Peter and James and his brother John and led them up a high mountain, by themselves. 2 And he was transfigured before them, and his face shone like the sun, and his clothes became dazzling white. 3 Suddenly there appeared to them Moses and Elijah, talking with him. 4 Then Peter said to Jesus, "Lord, it is good for us to be here; if you wish, I[a] will make three dwellings[b] here, one for you, one for Moses, and one for Elijah." 5 While he was still speaking, suddenly a bright cloud overshadowed them, and from the cloud a voice said, "This is my Son, the Beloved;[c] with him I am well pleased; listen to him!" 6 When the disciples heard this, they fell to the ground and were overcome by fear. 7 But Jesus came and touched them, saying, "Get up and do not be afraid." 8 And when they looked up, they saw no one except Jesus himself alone. 9 As they were coming down the mountain, Jesus ordered them, "Tell no one about the vision until after the Son of Man has been raised from the dead."

Tonight's a big night. Do you know that tonight is when our towns and cities are their safest? Tonight, for a few hours, there will be less crime committed than any other night of the year. Yep, even the criminals will be watching the Superbowl! Well, I don't know for sure if lower crime statistics is true or if it's just an urban myth but certainly there'll be lots of folks glued to their televisions sets tonight. How many of you are planning on watching the game? See? How many of you have already got your snacks organized? How many are planning a trip to Walmart soon as the service is over? I thought so!

> [pause]

Well, it'll be exciting alright. Now, for those of you who are football fans, please be patient, this next bit is going to be a tad boring for you. For those of you for whom professional football isn't at the top of your daily concerns, this year, the final game is between the New England Patriots and the New York Giants. The Patriots have a chance to do something that's only been done once before - win every single game in a season including the Super Bowl! But it's really going to be close - these two played at the end of the season and the Giants nearly won. So it's not at all clear who'll be the champions, notwithstanding the spread of 12 points in favor of New England. I guess we'll all just have to wait and see what happens tonight.

We do like a champion though, don't we? We want to be close to the champion - that's why everyone flocks around the winner at the Indy 500 or any other big event. We like to be close to that glory, that brightness. You watch - when they hold up the Lombardi trophy, it will sparkle and glitter in the light of all the photographers' flashes at the end of the game.

Not to drift too far afield, but - I won a race once. Yes, back in my youth, I had a race car, a Formula Ford and I raced it for a couple of years - until it used up all my money and my credit cards! But one time - I won! It was - amazing. My friends were delighted and we surely enjoyed the bright shine of glory. I lived on that event for several years. You see? The shine and applause and glory are heady, wonderful things that attract us like a moth to a porch light in the summertime.

So when the trophy goes to the winners tonight, we'll be watching, we'll feel great if it's our favorite team that wins. And the winner will be able to have their day, they'll be able to have things their way - at least for a while. And I think that's one of the reasons we like a winner, if we're on their side, we get to be right for a while too. We get to say, "I told you so!" We get to have it our way, at least vicariously. And that feels good; it always feels good to be on the side of the winners, doesn't it?

But what about the poor losers? They'll get a nod tonight but don't worry, all the glory will go to the winners. The losers will be pushed aside, overlooked, relegated to "2nd place" - losers. That's part of the problem with this sort of view of glory - it leads to 'us' versus 'them', winners versus losers. And, of course, the winners get things their way. If I'm a winner, I get to say, "I'm right." I get to say God is on *my* side.

And that's a real big problem I have with this text.

You see, if we equate 'transfiguration' with 'winning', then Jesus is the great winner, he's our hero, our knight in shining armor, our victorious leader - and we get to say what's right and what's wrong. And he looks like the winner, doesn't he? His face is shining like the sun and his clothes sparkle with a holy whiteness! You watch tonight - when they focus on the winners, they'll be lit up and shining too.

But that's not what transfiguration is, not by a long shot. No, transfiguration is really something being revealed, something that was there all along - but stays hidden - for some reason. Why would you do that? Why would someone give up all the glory if it was in them? Why would someone willingly give someone else the glory, the limelight - the Nike endorsements and Wheaties box covers?

Can you feel the tension that creates? This isn't about winning and losing - there's no tension there, someone wins - and someone loses. But this - this transfiguration is about the tension between glory and service. Because what else can you call it when someone's focus is on another? It's almost like a slave - someone who has to serve someone else. When you're in that place, your thoughts and actions are all about making your boss look good. Your attention is all on doing whatever the master says you need to do. Now, the Master is right - but it's not at all like losing, is it? No, I don't think it is.

You know what I think? I think that's the tension that's going on in this text. On the one hand, Jesus' real nature is revealed, he's transfigured. But like a cloud covering the sun, in the next instant, Jesus seems - just - normal. Jesus looks just like he did before they ever walked up that mountain. He's still just the one who heals the sick, the one who eats with tax collectors and sinners, the one who scandalizes the powers that be by feeding and healing people on the sabbath - the one who deals with women as equals - in public!

He's the one who serves everybody else. But he's - God!

> [*show the tension by acting it out*]

You see? Can you feel that tension? When we get caught up just in the glory side, it's way too easy to relieve that tension by making Jesus a winner - and not a savior.

> [*pause*]

I've always felt the apostle Paul had a great way of explaining this in his letter to the Philippians. In Philippians 2:5-8, the verses known as the Philippians Hymn, Paul lays it out:

> *Let the same mind be in you that was in Christ Jesus,*
> *who, though he was in the form of God,*
>   *did not regard equality with God*
>   *as something to be exploited,*
> *but emptied himself,*
>   *taking the form of a slave,*
>   *being born in human likeness.*
> *And being found in human form,*
>   *he humbled himself*
>   *and became obedient to the point of death—*
>   *even death on a cross.*

Obedient to who? To God! Jesus never takes the winners' role; he never says *I'm* right. His focus, his attention is always on his Master - God. Jesus is a servant, a steward - a slave. You know, we read this text in Matthew and it's so easy to get caught up in the glory, you can almost let the most important line in the whole text slip by. It's just three words. "Listen to him." It's not - 'praise him', or 'build him a house' or 'give him an award' or 'get his autograph', no it's "listen to him!"

And just who is it that tells us this? God. So do we listen? I don't know. Sometimes we do, I think. But here's what I think. That tension exists or at least the possibility for that tension is always there, even in the hymns we sing. Take the wonderful Praise song I taught the kids last week - "Awesome God":

> "Our God is an awesome God
> He reigns from heaven above
> With wisdom, power, and love
> Our God is an awesome God!"[1]

Now, hear this one I'll begin teaching them next week:

> "Make me a servant, humble and meek
> Lord, let me lift up those who are weak
> And may the prayer of my heart always be
> Make me a servant, make me a servant
> Make me a servant today"[2]

If we only sing about the blazing glory - we make one a winner and the other a loser - and we lose that tension. No, we always need to sing both blazing glory AND stewardship because it's only in the two together that we truly understand that our salvation is deeply held in the tension between them. Our salvation is in Jesus, the one who lives comfortably in that tension.

"Listen to him!"

That is good news, indeed! Amen.

---

[1] *Awesome God* on Winds of Heaven, Stuff of Earth, R. Mullins, 1988.
[2] *Make Me A Servant,* Kelly Willard, CCM Music/Willing Heart Music, 1982.

Saved from Ourselves
John 3:1-17

3 Now there was a Pharisee named Nicodemus, a leader of the Jews. 2 He came to Jesus by night and said to him, "Rabbi, we know that you are a teacher who has come from God; for no one can do these signs that you do apart from the presence of God." 3 Jesus answered him, "Very truly, I tell you, no one can see the kingdom of God without being born from above." 4 Nicodemus said to him, "How can anyone be born after having grown old? Can one enter a second time into the mother's womb and be born?" 5 Jesus answered, "Very truly, I tell you, no one can enter the kingdom of God without being born of water and Spirit. 6 What is born of the flesh is flesh, and what is born of the Spirit is spirit. 7 Do not be astonished that I said to you, 'You must be born from above.' 8 The wind blows where it chooses, and you hear the sound of it, but you do not know where it comes from or where it goes. So it is with everyone who is born of the Spirit." 9 Nicodemus said to him, "How can these things be?" 10 Jesus answered him, "Are you a teacher of Israel, and yet you do not understand these things? 11 "Very truly, I tell you, we speak of what we know and testify to what we have seen; yet you do not receive our testimony. 12 If I have told you about earthly things and you do not believe; how can you believe if I tell you about heavenly things? 13 No one has ascended into heaven except the one who descended from heaven, the Son of Man. 14 And just as Moses lifted up the serpent in the wilderness, so must the Son of Man be lifted up, 15 that whoever believes in him may have eternal life.

16 "For God so loved the world that he gave his only Son, so that everyone who believes in him may not perish but may have eternal life. 17 "Indeed, God did not send the Son into the world to condemn the world, but in order that the world might be saved through him.

Well. Here we are in the gospel attributed to John. It's different, isn't it? It's sort of like the difference between watching a sitcom on commercial TV versus a show on Public TV. John's - more cerebral, more philosophical. The metaphors are different and the author doesn't even mention many of the narrative elements the other synoptic gospels do. So we can't just switch from Matthew, the gospel we've been in for the last three weeks, without some background work. The way Matthew says things is just plain different from the way John does!

For example, listen to what Matthew puts on the lips of John the Baptist when the Pharisees and Sadducees came to him to be baptized: "You brood of vipers! Who warned you to flee from the wrath to come?" The gospel of John, on the other hand, says, "This is the testimony given by John the Baptist when the Jews sent priests and Levites from Jerusalem to ask him, 'Who are you?' He confessed and did not deny it but confessed, "I am not the Messiah." And they asked him, "What then? Are you Elijah?" You see? One is Fox news, the other, NPR radio news.

And the final words are different too. In Matthew, John the Baptist says, "I baptize you with water for repentance but one who is more powerful than I is coming after me; I am not worthy to carry his sandals." Now listen to what the gospel of John reports: "John the Baptist answered them, 'I baptize with water. Among you stands one whom you do not know, the one who is coming after me; I am not worthy to untie the thong of his sandals."

See? In Matthew, the priests seem to know who John the Baptist is and what's coming; they're going to get baptized. In John, they don't have a clue. This will be important for our text today as well. There's another really big difference too. The two gospels start with entirely different perspectives. Matthew gives us a lengthy, detailed account of Jesus' genealogy and a story of Jesus' birth; John does something entirely different - well, just listen to what John says: [*read John 1:1-5, 10-14*]

This difference is huge. In the gospel attributed to John, human Jesus and divine God are pulled together: "In the beginning was the Word, and the Word was with God and the Word was God. And the Word became flesh and lived among us, and we have seen his glory, the glory *as of* a father's only son." You see? John doesn't think of Jesus as literally God's son, no, for John, Jesus and God are the same but how can we describe God's love? Well, it's the kind of love that a parent has for an only child. In the ancient, biblical, patriarchal context - a father for an only son. When John says, 'son of God', he's trying to convey a sense of how God loves us - it's not genealogical or a statement of heredity.

Okay, take a deep breath - we're movin' on!

So let's sum up what we've got so far. In John, the characters generally don't get who Jesus is so it's like they're talking apples and Jesus is talking oranges - they just don't get what Jesus is saying. Do any of you recall a rather popular book from several years ago, *Men are from Mars, Women are from Venus*? It's like that. Second, as far as John is concerned, Jesus is in God and God is in Jesus. Period.

Got it? Whew! I think we've made it through the rough stuff. Don't worry, this'll all come together as we seek to understand our text for today. Umm, now I've lost track of that... oh yes! John 3:1-17. Actually, the whole first part of this is the setup for the well-known verses 3:16-17. But it fits what we already know about John. Nicodemus can't understand Jesus' teaching -

because he's only seeing flesh - real birth - so how can anyone be born twice? But Jesus is talking about spirit - it's different. It's a setup for the key verses, this whole discussion about Nicodemus and flesh vs. spirit. We should be on our toes to watch out for misunderstanding, i.e., we'll think one thing but the author will mean something else.

And that brings us to John 3:16 and 17: "For God so loved the world that he gave his only son, so that everyone who believes in him may not perish but may have eternal life. Indeed, God did not send the Son into the world to condemn the world, but in order that the world might be saved through him."

[*pause*]

Have you ever watched the way Perrin and Avihenda run to their mom and dad, just run up and lean against them? Or the way Abby leans on her older brother Matt, sort of safe in his shadow? When I was a kid, I used to love coming home from school and getting to tell my mom and dad some of the things I'd learned at school that day as we sat around the kitchen table having dinner together. It never crossed my mind that these elementary things might be boring to them, that they might have more important things to worry about. I trusted completely and absolutely that they were interested in me and my day. And then, when I was in my teen years, I remember my folks telling me that some idea or plan I had cooked up was not so good - and I'd change my mind - they'd always been right before so I could trust their judgement and experience on these matters too.

Now, before you go thinking I was some kind of saintly kid, let me assure you that there were plenty of times I went right ahead without consulting my folks - that's when I found the truth in the saying, "Experience is what you get when you don't get what you want!"

But you know what I'm talking about, don't you? That complete trust and faith that we had in our parents or maybe a good friend. We just flat knew our thoughts and dreams and even doubts would be safe with them. That's the kind of trust and faith the gospel of John is talking about when it says, "so that everyone who *believes* in him." The greek word that gets translated as 'believes' is *pisteuo* - it's defined in Strong's Concordance as "to have faith (in, upon, or with respect to, a person or thing); by implication to entrust (especially one's spiritual well-being to Christ): - believe, believer, commit (to trust), put in trust with." That's the weight of 'believes' in this text. That's the way we're called to *believe* in Jesus, in God. "Believe" - that's the first keyword in this text.

The other keyword in our text today is 'saved'. The greek word used here is *sozo* and it means, "to save, i.e., deliver or protect; heal, preserve, save, do well, be [or make] whole." That makes sense, doesn't it?

[*pause; sigh*]

But I can't help it, my goofy mind always comes up with questions. In this case, the text says, "so that *the world* might be *saved*." 'Saved' from what? Or from whom? It doesn't say, "so that *you* might be saved or *I* might be saved...' no, it says, 'the world...' From what is the world to be 'delivered, protected, healed, preserved, made whole'?

Now don't spread this around, but I think it's from us. I think it's from *us* that the world needs to be saved. I think we're the ones responsible for making this world - the place, the people, everything - a wonderful place, a garden of Eden, so to speak. I think it's *us* that we need to be saved from! We get so caught up in worrying about our own salvation, we totally miss what God's been after us to do - well - since the beginning. In Genesis 2:15, it says, "The LORD God took the man and put him in the garden of Eden to *till it and keep it*." I looked up the definitions for those words, 'till' and 'keep' - they mean 'to watch over, to guard thoroughly, i.e. protect; to preserve, *save*." The same as the word 'saved' in our text here in the gospel of John!

Now, listen to 3:16 and 17 with our new understanding: "For God so loved the world, like a father loves an only son, that God came into the world, so that everyone who *believes* in God may not perish but may have eternal life. Indeed, God did not come into the world to condemn the world, but in order to help us *save* the world."

Hmmmmph. So God sent Jesus - God - into the world to show us how to save the world - from us? But what about us? When do we - "get saved?" Are you ready for the best part of this whole, confusing text? We already are saved! The whole point is that if we turn away, repent from belief in ourselves, to *believe* in God as revealed to us in Jesus who loves us with a love like that of a parent for an only child, if we trust like a child, we won't perish but have eternal life! God's given us that - we don't earn it. Did any of us 'earn' the love of our parents? No! We trusted them, we *believed* in them. That's the way Jesus loved God. If we believe - trust - have faith in - God/Jesus, we'll be able to 'save' the world just as God's asked us to all along. Or, we can continue to live in the world we create all by ourselves.

[*pause*]

We can have that kind of world, an Eden-like world - the kingdom of God. That's the world we're made for. Everything looks different when we realize just how much God loves us. That's why we recite these particular verses each week during communion. We remember how Jesus loved and stand amazed that we're loved like that. We remember how Jesus lived and died and we have reason to think we can live like that too! We can *live* in a world where justice comes first. We can *live* in a world where the poor and weak are taken care of. We can *live* in a world where all have enough and where the stranger isn't feared but honored and offered hospitality. We can *live* in a world where love really rules, where love comes first, where life comes first.

We can live in a world like that - because God loves us like that.

And that is good news, indeed! Amen.

A Solitary Shell Game
John 9:1-41

9 As he walked along, he saw a man blind from birth. 2 His disciples asked him, "Rabbi, who sinned, this man or his parents, that he was born blind?" 3 Jesus answered, "Neither this man nor his parents sinned; he was born blind so that God's works might be revealed in him. 4 We must work the works of him who sent me while it is day; night is coming when no one can work. 5 As long as I am in the world, I am the light of the world." 6 When he had said this, he spat on the ground and made mud with the saliva and spread the mud on the man's eyes, 7 saying to him, "Go, wash in the pool of Siloam" (which means Sent). Then he went and washed and came back able to see. 8 The neighbors and those who had seen him before as a beggar began to ask, "Is this not the man who used to sit and beg?" 9 Some were saying, "It is he." Others were saying, "No, but it is someone like him." He kept saying, "I am the man." 10 But they kept asking him, "Then how were your eyes opened?" 11 He answered, "The man called Jesus made mud, spread it on my eyes, and said to me, 'Go to Siloam and wash.' Then I went and washed and received my sight." 12 They said to him, "Where is he?" He said, "I do not know."

13 They brought to the Pharisees the man who had formerly been blind. 14 Now it was a sabbath day when Jesus made the mud and opened his eyes. 15 Then the Pharisees also began to ask him how he had received his sight. He said to them, "He put mud on my eyes. Then I washed, and now I see." 16 Some of the Pharisees said, "This man is not from God, for he does not observe the sabbath." But others said, "How can a man who is a sinner perform such signs?" And they were divided. 17 So they said again to the blind man, "What do you say about him? It was your eyes he opened." He said, "He is a prophet."

18 The Jews did not believe that he had been blind and had received his sight until they called the parents of the man who had received his sight 19 and asked them, "Is this your son, who you say was born blind? How then does he now see?" 20 His parents answered, "We know that this is our son, and that he was born blind; 21 but we do not know how it is that now he sees, nor do we know who opened his eyes. Ask him; he is of age. He will speak for himself." 22 His parents said this because they were afraid of the Jews; for the Jews had already agreed that anyone who confessed Jesus to be the Messiah would be put out of the synagogue. 23 Therefore his parents said, "He is of age; ask him."

24 So for the second time they called the man who had been blind, and they said to him, "Give glory to God! We know that this man is a sinner." 25 He answered, "I do not know whether he is a sinner. One thing I do know, that though I was blind, now I see." 26 They said to him, "What did he do to you? How did he open your eyes?" 27 He answered them, "I have told you already, and you would not listen. Why do you want to hear it again? Do you also want to become his disciples?" 28 Then they reviled him, saying,

"You are his disciple, but we are disciples of Moses. 29 We know that God has spoken to Moses, but as for this man, we do not know where he comes from." 30 The man answered, "Here is an astonishing thing! You do not know where he comes from, and yet he opened my eyes. 31 We know that God does not listen to sinners, but he does listen to one who worships him and obeys his will. 32 Never since the world began has it been heard that anyone opened the eyes of a person born blind. 33 If this man were not from God, he could do nothing." 34 They answered him, "You were born entirely in sins, and are you trying to teach us?" And they drove him out.

35 Jesus heard that they had driven him out, and when he found him, he said, "Do you believe in the Son of Man?" 36 He answered, "And who is he, sir? Tell me, so that I may believe in him." 37 Jesus said to him, "You have seen him, and the one speaking with you is he." 38 He said, "Lord, I believe." And he worshiped him. 39 Jesus said, "I came into this world for judgment so that those who do not see may see, and those who do see may become blind." 40 Some of the Pharisees near him heard this and said to him, "Surely we are not blind, are we?" 41 Jesus said to them, "If you were blind, you would not have sin. But now that you say, 'We see,' your sin remains.

[Props: table with three cups turned upside down. Play the game by moving the cups around then leave them unturned...]

I preached down at my Alma Mater this past week. I preached on this text from the gospel attributed to John. Boy, I wish I'd taken a class on John back when I was a student! This gospel is dense and confusing and - well - difficult, I think. There are clear references to the dualism that was so much a part of Plato yet what the author does with it is downright scandalous. The very thought of the Word, the logos, unchanging - residing in mortal, corruptible, flesh... *[shiver - yyeeeewwww!]* It'd make a gnostic roll over in his grave! Thank goodness there's no such deviousness in our text today. Thank goodness all we've got in this text is a simple case of 'now you see it, now you don't' - a sort of cosmic shell game.

You remember the old shell games, don't you? The operator has three cups and a pea or anything small enough to fit under the cup - or maybe it's done with three cards. You see the pea or card or whatever, then the operator shuffles them all around and you have to try to follow the right one and pick it to win the prize. Shouldn't be too hard - we're watching the whole time - we know what we saw, don't we? Yeah, right! Why do you think the operator has such a big smile?

What we see and don't see is a fascinating question, isn't it? I know it is for my wife and me. I can be standing right in the middle of the kitchen with all the cupboards wide open hollering, "Where's the - put in here whatever it is you can't find either! - and Patty will calmly walk in, pick it out, and gently hand it to me. Particularly if it's something in 'Tupperware Hell' - I can never find anything down there!

You see, don't you? We might be looking in the same direction - but we don't 'see' the same things. I think that's maybe what's going on in this story in our text for today - everyone's sort of looking in the same direction, but they're not seeing the same things. And nobody's seeing what Jesus is seeing - except maybe the blind man.

The real problem is, *I'm* supposed to be preaching on this very text - bringing you some 'insight' into a text about - sight. Can you spell 'irony'? And to make matters more burdensome, as a Disciple of Christ, our tradition calls us to receive "the light of scripture." (from the Preamble to the Design of the Christian Church (Disciples of Christ)) Well, I suppose I'd better get started then.

But before that, you know something that's just really bothered me about this text? I did a narrative analysis - the character with the most lines is the blind man - the pharisees are not too far behind - they're the two main characters; and all the other characters have a say along the way too. So what bothers me is that in this whole long story - nobody tells the blind man how great it is that his sight's been restored! Nobody says 'WOW!' Nobody hugs him, nobody says what a wonderful thing this is. Isn't that odd? How could they all miss that? What did they think they were seeing?

It's funny how people see different things. And I don't mean like when I can't see something right in front of me in the kitchen, no, this is more like when we're all looking at one thing - and we don't 'see' the same thing. It's like a plantation owner and an abolitionist in the middle 1800s looking at an African slave. One saw a piece of property while the other saw a human being. It's like a parent and a teenager in the early 60s when the Beatles came to America - one saw (and heard) the devil's music while the other danced and screamed for joy!

Sometimes, we think we 'see' things, we think we 'know' what's going on - and we're just flat wrong. How many of us - white, middle class Americans - stranded on the side of the road with a flat tire as we head home from a night meeting, would see an approaching African American or Hispanic man and wonder whether he's there to help us or to mug us? Yet we 'know' we're not racist, right? How many of us see someone dressed in a head scarf and kaftan and think of '911', yet we 'know' we're not xenophobic and intolerant, don't we?

You see, don't you? We let ourselves get blinded all the time by our prejudices, our self-centeredness, our personal desires and greed, and our self-doubts - our blind spots. That's what's going on in this dialog between the blind man and the religious authorities. All the blind man 'sees' is "I was blind - now I see." But the neighbors and his family and the religious leaders all see something else. The neighbors 'know' he's been blind since birth - and there's no cure so it simply can't be him. His parents 'know' the religious authorities will throw them out of the synagogue, out of their community, if they defy them so they virtually dis-own their own son in order to 'see' a way to save themselves. And the Pharisees 'know' that he's a sinner and they 'know' they know more than this sinner does! So they throw him out - just as his parents 'knew' they would.

But none of them, not a single person, sees what the blind man saw - "I was blind but now I see." Yeah, it's funny how people see different things. It's like a poor itinerant preacher hanging on a cross and the mob of people who put him there - one sees the people - all God's children - and forgives them; the others see a freak and a nobody who's a troublemaker.

"I was blind - but now - I see."

> [*pause*]

Well. If 'seeing' isn't maybe so clear, how would it be to be blind? One of the last things the author of John puts on Jesus' lips in this narrative is the statement, "I came into this world for judgement so that those who do not see may see and those who do see may become blind." "Those who do see - may become blind."

Some time ago, I wrote a song titled, "Blind Like Jesus". The chorus is:

> "O God, make me blind like Jesus, so I can finally see
> See my brothers and sisters, living in harmony
> Blind to race, gender, creed, sexual identity
> Blind like Jesus, O God, help me be."[1]

So what is it I need to be made blind to? Or maybe a better way to ask this is what are my blind spots? I need to see that my egotistical belief that I'm smart and know what I'm talking about is a blind spot. I need to see that my self-doubts and fears that keep me from helping strangers are blind spots. I need to see that my judgmental nature that makes me holler at other drivers, the judgments that make me think less of anyone simply on the basis of what I 'see' about them - how well dressed they are or how they smell - is really a blind spot.

I need to be made blind so I can see with the eyes of my heart. This is nothing new, of course. The great Doctor of the church, Teresa of Avila, said it better than I when she wrote, "Let us strive, then, always to look at the virtues and the good qualities which we find in others, and to keep our own grievous sins before our own eyes so that we may be blind to their defects."[2]

The more blind I become to others' defects, the more I can see with the eyes of my heart.

What would it be like to lose our sight? What would it be like to become blind?

I have a friend, Donnie, who is HIV positive. It's not surprising to understand that he wasn't happy to learn this diagnosis, that it made him angry. He became mean-tempered, short, and rude with everyone. He was judgmental and hateful to people who were different from him. One might've even considered him racist.

All of that would be discouraging enough but it got worse. As a complication from his illnesses, he went blind! Now he was really mad - for a while. Then, one day when a neighbor brought him his mail, he said, "Thank you." and meant it. He didn't offer a snide comment or put-down. The next week a few people stopped by for a visit and Donnie was so happy he never even noticed one was African American and one Jewish. As far as he could 'see', they were friends and he was grateful for their presence. Life became a blessing. Even though his sight was gone, he began to 'see' joy and happiness even in the midst of his illness.

I need to be made blind so I can begin to see like my friend, Donnie.

> [*move to the cups and rearrange them one final time*]

All this time, I thought I knew where the pea was, which cup held the prize. But it's just a shell game - there never really was anything there [*turn cups over*]. A solitary shell game I played with myself.

"I was blind - but now - I see."

That is good news, indeed! Amen.

---

[1] *Blind Like Jesus* on Messengers, S. R. Taylor, 2000.

[2] Avila, T. *The Life of Teresa of Jesus - The Autobiography of Teresa of Avila*, translated and edited by E. Allison Peers, (New York, NY: Image Books Doubleday), 1991, p. 142.

What's Death Got to Do with It?
John 11:1-45

11 *Now a certain man was ill, Lazarus of Bethany, the village of Mary and her sister Martha. 2 Mary was the one who anointed the Lord with perfume and wiped his feet with her hair; her brother Lazarus was ill. 3 So the sisters sent a message to Jesus, "Lord, he whom you love is ill." 4 But when Jesus heard it, he said, "This illness does not lead to death; rather it is for God's glory, so that the Son of God may be glorified through it." 5 Accordingly, though Jesus loved Martha and her sister and Lazarus, 6 after having heard that Lazarus was ill, he stayed two days longer in the place where he was.*

7 Then after this he said to the disciples, "Let us go to Judea again." 8 The disciples said to him, "Rabbi, the Jews were just now trying to stone you, and are you going there again?" 9 Jesus answered, "Are there not twelve hours of daylight? Those who walk during the day do not stumble, because they see the light of this world. 10 But those who walk at night stumble, because the light is not in them." 11 After saying this, he told them, "Our friend Lazarus has fallen asleep, but I am going there to awaken him." 12 The disciples said to him, "Lord, if he has fallen asleep, he will be all right." 13 Jesus, however, had been speaking about his death, but they thought that he was referring merely to sleep. 14 Then Jesus told them plainly, "Lazarus is dead. 15 For your sake I am glad I was not there, so that you may believe. But let us go to him." 16 Thomas, who was called the Twin, said to his fellow disciples, "Let us also go, that we may die with him."

17 When Jesus arrived, he found that Lazarus had already been in the tomb four days. 18 Now Bethany was near Jerusalem, some two miles away, 19 and many of the Jews had come to Martha and Mary to console them about their brother. 20 When Martha heard that Jesus was coming, she went and met him, while Mary stayed at home. 21 Martha said to Jesus, "Lord, if you had been here, my brother would not have died. 22 But even now I know that God will give you whatever you ask of him." 23 Jesus said to her, "Your brother will rise again." 24 Martha said to him, "I know that he will rise again in the resurrection on the last day." 25 Jesus said to her, "I am the resurrection and the life. Those who believe in me, even though they die, will live, 26 and everyone who lives and believes in me will never die. Do you believe this?" 27 She said to him, "Yes, Lord, I believe that you are the Messiah, the Son of God, the one coming into the world."

28 When she had said this, she went back and called her sister Mary, and told her privately, "The Teacher is here and is calling for you." 29 And when she heard it, she got up quickly and went to him. 30 Now Jesus had not yet come to the village but was still at the place where Martha had met him. 31 The Jews who were with her in the house, consoling her, saw Mary get up quickly and go out. They followed her because they thought that she was going to the tomb to weep there. 32 When Mary came where Jesus was and saw him, she knelt at his feet and said to him, "Lord, if you had been here, my brother would not have died." 33 When Jesus saw her weeping, and the Jews who came with her also weeping, he was greatly disturbed in spirit and deeply moved. 34 He said, "Where have you laid him?" They said to him, "Lord, come and see." 35 Jesus began to weep. 36 So the Jews said, "See how he loved him!" 37 But some of them said, "Could not he who opened the eyes of the blind man have kept this man from dying?"

38 Then Jesus, again greatly disturbed, came to the tomb. It was a cave, and a stone was lying against it. 39 Jesus said, "Take away the stone." Martha, the sister of the dead man, said to him, "Lord, already there is a stench because he has been dead four days." 40 Jesus said to her, "Did I not tell you that if you believed, you would see the glory of God?" 41 So they took away the stone. And Jesus looked upward and said, "Father, I thank you for having heard me. 42 I knew that you always hear me, but I have said this for the sake of the crowd standing here, so that they may believe that you sent me." 43 When he had said this, he cried with a loud voice, "Lazarus, come out!" 44 The dead man came out, his hands and feet bound with strips of cloth, and his face wrapped in a cloth. Jesus said to them, "Unbind him, and let him go." 45 Many of the Jews therefore, who had come with Mary and had seen what Jesus did, believed in him.

Death. We don't want to face it. Death. We don't want to talk about it. Death. A part of all of our lives someday. It is so troublesome to us that we make all sorts of euphemisms for it:

- Cross over
- pass away
- meet your maker
- gone to a final resting place
- gone to be with God

And, of course, there are those euphemisms that try to lighten the seriousness of the moment:

- bite the dust
- pushing up daisies
- sleep with the fishes

And of course, there's one famous for a recent movie title, the ever popular 'kicked the bucket'. I did a quick search and found a website with over 1000 of these euphemisms for death!

I'm sure you have some yourself. Why is death such a touchy subject? Well, most likely because it scares us! No one knows what is on the other side yet all of us know we'll find out someday. Of course, as Christians, we believe in Jesus' death, burial, and resurrection and how that shows us we're saved, too. But even facing a loved one's *impending* death is difficult. Our loved ones don't find it easy either. Listen to this story from the book, *Final Gifts*, by Maggie Callanan and Patricia Kelley, two hospice nurses:

"When I arrived the next afternoon Julia's daughter Jane, a former nurse who was providing much of her mother's care, was weeping in the kitchen. Julia had extensive and inoperable lung cancer.

"It's so hard to cope with this," Jane said. "Last night my mother was saying the doctors never know anything, and that she'll be fine if she can only start eating again. That made Dad really mad; he yelled at her and then stormed out of the house. He didn't come back for hours, and when he did, he'd been drinking. This morning my sister Sally calls to talk about getting in touch with a funeral home, and she can't figure out why I can't stop crying. Then my brother calls from California to tell me about some new chemotherapy, he wants to know if Mom's doctor knows about it. Is this family going crazy, or is it just me?"

Jane realized she was grieving and depressed but was grateful that she at least was dealing with reality. She went over the reactions of others in the family.

"Mother's in denial but that won't last long," she said. "She's known for a while that she's getting worse; last week she even told me she doesn't want to go on like this. Dad, of course, will be hopeless. He's always hiding his feelings behind angry words and drink."

Then she laughed and pointed to the heap of sodden tissues on the kitchen counter. "But this generation isn't doing too well, either," Jane said. "John's a real wheeler-dealer. I bet he thinks he can find Mom a deal that'll fix everything. And Sally - she'll stay calm, controlled, and accepting for a while, then fall apart when something changes."

A few days later, Jane had an update. "We all changed roles," she said. "I yelled at Dad for drinking. He and Mom had a long talk about funeral plans; Mom had him call the priest. Father Wheeler came over and they put together a ceremony, and Dad's been crying all evening. Now Mom's working on a list of what she wants the grandchildren to have," Jane continued. "She collects music boxes, and she's tagging her favorites so we know who gets which one. Sally telephoned the doctor to see if that new drug might work, and John called to say he hadn't slept the last few nights, worrying that he might not see Mom before she died. So he's coming home this weekend."[1]

[*pause*]

Sounds familiar, doesn't it? We've all experienced this roller coaster - maybe some time ago - maybe recently. So we read this text about Lazarus and we know how Mary and Martha and the family are feeling. We feel and empathize with their pain and grief in a flash as we share in those days approaching Lazarus' death and then immediately afterwards. We, too, get angry thinking about the way Jesus delayed and didn't get there in time. And even Jesus feels this pain we have, he weeps and is overcome too.

Lazarus is dead.

[*pause*]

What's really ironic is here we are talking all about death - and that's not what this text is actually about! *We* want to make death a big deal - the main character - but it's not, at least not in this story! I did a narrative analysis again and this week, it's Jesus who's the main character, the one with the most lines. The next most important is the narrator! Even Mary and Martha only have small parts. And Lazarus? He doesn't have any lines at all. And yet, we try to make him the focal point. This story is such a reversal, we almost can't even see it. For us, life precedes death. Not in this story. No, Lazarus is dead from the beginning, even if most of the characters don't know it, Jesus does. And he's indifferent to it. For you see, he knows this story is the ultimate reversal - it goes from death - to life!

From death - to life!

And we almost can't go there. Martha and Mary can't go there, at least not initially. They both chastise Jesus with the same words, "Lord, if you had been there, my brother would not have died." They think he should've come sooner to help their brother.

You know, I had a marvelous example of this sort of misunderstanding once. I was at a production of the play, Dracula, that was done in the round; there was no backstage. Rather, the actors stood in the shadows at the edges of the audience while the action shifted; then they'd quietly move to their next scene. But it didn't work for one little boy. In the scene where the doctor's fiancée` is left alone while they go hunt Dracula, the doctor tells her to be sure to lock the doors and windows. Then the actors left the scene coming to stand only a few feet from where we were sitting. She's still on the lit set right in front of us. Of course, she doesn't lock the windows and here comes Dracula to get her. However, the little boy didn't 'see' that. He saw the young woman being attacked - he saw her 'fianceé' standing just few feet away - and couldn't help himself. He turned to the actor trying to fade into the shadows and said, "Well, don't just stand there - go help her!"

[*pause*]

I think that's how Mary and Martha want to respond to Jesus. They can't see that death could lead to life. They can't see that Jesus sees beyond them to life in God eternal and that, through him, we, too, can live in life eternal. Jesus doesn't weep because Lazarus is dead, no, he weeps because of the pain and suffering his friends, Mary and Martha, are experiencing. For Jesus, this has been a story of death to life all along. It's what he's been preaching all through this gospel, "Do you believe?" If we believe in Jesus, then we, too, can live - in Jesus, 'even though we die, we will live'.

This sense of Jesus with us and in us and through us expressed in the pivotal verse 26a, "and everyone who lives and believes *in me* will never die," was captured most eloquently by St. Patrick long, long ago. Hear this excerpt from a prayer by the Irish Saint:

> Christ to shield me today
> Against poison, against burning,
> Against drowning, against wounding,
> So that there may come to me abundance of reward.
> Christ with me, Christ before me, Christ behind me,
> Christ in me, Christ beneath me, Christ above me,
> Christ on my right, Christ on my left,
> Christ when I lie down, Christ when I sit down, Christ when I arise,
> Christ in the heart of every man who thinks of me,
> Christ in the mouth of everyone who speaks of me,
> Christ in every eye that sees me,
> Christ in every ear that hears me.
>
> I arise today
> Through a mighty strength, the invocation of the Trinity,
> Through belief in the Threeness,
> Through confession of the oneness,
> Of the Creator of Creation.

This is the Jesus who calls to Lazarus, "Come Out!" This is what Jesus means when he says, "I am the resurrection and the life." Lazarus' being raised from the dead is just a mere trailer, a teaser for the real thing to come and this is the good news we proclaim and will celebrate loudly in two weeks on Easter morning! From death to life! Do you believe?

Amen.

---

[1] *Final Gifts*, Maggie Callanan and Patricia Kelley, Simon & Schuster, 1992.

See, It's Like This...
Matthew 21:1-11; Psalm 118:1-2, 19-29

21 When they had come near Jerusalem and had reached Bethphage, at the Mount of Olives, Jesus sent two disciples, 2 saying to them, "Go into the village ahead of you, and immediately you will find a donkey tied, and a colt with her; untie them and bring them to me. 3 If anyone says anything to you, just say this, 'The Lord needs them.' And he will send them immediately." 4 This took place to fulfill what had been spoken through the prophet, saying,

5 "Tell the daughter of Zion, Look, your king is coming to you, humble, and mounted on a donkey, and on a colt, the foal of a donkey."

6 The disciples went and did as Jesus had directed them; 7 they brought the donkey and the colt, and put their cloaks on them, and he sat on them. 8 A very large crowd spread their cloaks on the road, and others cut branches from the trees and spread them on the road. 9 The crowds that went ahead of him and that followed were shouting,

"Hosanna to the Son of David! Blessed is the one who comes in the name of the Lord!

Hosanna in the highest heaven!"

10 When he entered Jerusalem, the whole city was in turmoil, asking, "Who is this?" 11 The crowds were saying, "This is the prophet Jesus from Nazareth in Galilee."

A Song of Victory

1 O give thanks to the Lord, for he is good.
 his steadfast love endures forever!
2 Let Israel say,
 "His steadfast love endures forever."

19 Open to me the gates of righteousness,
 that I may enter through them
 and give thanks to the Lord.
20 This is the gate of the Lord.
 the righteous shall enter through it.
21 I thank you that you have answered me
 and have become my salvation.
22 The stone that the builders rejected
 has become the chief cornerstone.
23 This is the Lord's doing.

it is marvelous in our eyes.
24 This is the day that the Lord has made.
   let us rejoice and be glad in it.
25 Save us, we beseech you, O Lord!
   O Lord, we beseech you, give us success!
26 Blessed is the one who comes in the name of the Lord.
   We bless you from the house of the Lord.
27 The Lord is God,
   and he has given us light.
Bind the festal procession with branches,
   up to the horns of the altar.
28 You are my God, and I will give thanks to you.
   you are my God; I will extol you.
29 O give thanks to the Lord, for he is good,
   for his steadfast love endures forever.

How many of you have ever been to or watched a parade? Um Hmmm, quite a lot of us then. They're really fun, aren't they? Of course, I guess the two most ubiquitous parades that all of us watch at some point are the Macy's Thanksgiving Day parade in New York and then the Tournament of Roses parade each January in Pasadena, CA. But they each have such different character, don't they?

Macy's Thanksgiving Day parade has all those huge balloons. There's always 'Charlie Brown' and 'Big Bird' - wonderful characters but perhaps the most famous and longest running are 'Snoopy' and - anyone want to take a guess? 'Kermit'! 'Kermit the Frog'! But the parts I love the most are the little snippets from whatever hot shows are on Broadway. I love the music and the choreography; it makes me want to take Patty and I to New York sometime and see the parade firsthand and maybe take in a show ourselves.

On the other hand, California in January verses New York in November? I might want to head to sunny California! Afterall, that's why the Tournament of Roses parade got started - to showcase the region's terrific weather and blooming flowers while New York was covered in snow. And boy, do they use those flowers! I don't know about you but I think the Rose parade's always got the best floats. Beautiful designs, amazing technologies - but what a mess to clean up! Mike Rowe, on the TV show, 'Dirty Jobs', did a whole show on cleaning floats after these big parades. Of course, the technical job title was 'Parade Float Dismantler' a nice euphemism for shoveling dead flowers and rotten vegetables!

But what are the parades about? What do they mean to us? The Macy's parade always seems to me to be about a combination of commercial icons and Broadway advertisement sort of mixed up with memories of my Grandparents' house where I usually watched the parade - with the aroma of the turkey cooking in the kitchen just down the hall. The Rose parades? That's a bit like a warmup for the Rose Bowl and it's an excuse to stay in my pajamas and robe for a few more hours on New Year's Day! I suppose they're each like a picture of my childhood; I could easily say the Macy's Thanksgiving Day parade is like an old time black and white photo of my youth. No matter what else went on, there's always that warm undercurrent of memories of family and smells and rug textures backlit with the parade on the old Dumont TV set.

The Rose parade's more like my younger adult years - bright and flashy and exciting but rather naive and doomed to end at the hands of a 'Parade Float Dismantler'!

They're both metaphors for my life, my world, as it was, or is, depending on how far I want to take it. We use things like this to describe our lives. For example, I might say to you, 'My childhood with my grandparents was like watching a Thanksgiving Day parade waiting for the turkey to come out of the oven'. And those of you who watch that parade would have a fair idea of what it all means to me and you'd smile and nod your heads - because you'd have your own metaphor playing out in your head too. Yeah, I can see you smiling!

So why am I telling you all of this? Because the way we use metaphors *is* the way we describe our world. All I'd have to say is, 'My childhood was like a Macy's Thanksgiving Day parade!', and it would make you think; you'd have to play that out and see where it took you. You'd *have* to think about it. Metaphors do that - they say one thing is like another - but not exactly!

This is just the way Jesus taught throughout his whole ministry. He used parables - which are short, narrative, metaphors. Some are just one sentence long, for example: 'The kingdom of God is like a mustard seed.' - we all know that one - but what does it mean? You've got to think about it. The mustard plant is a weed - is Jesus trying to tell us the kingdom of God is a weed? Hmmmmph. You see? Parables don't give you answers - they make you ask questions; they make *you* figure it out.

That's what's happening in the Matthew text today. This whole entrance into Jerusalem is a parable. It's almost as if Jesus is acting out the kingdom of God. It's like he's saying, 'See? It's like this…' So it's like a parade - but not exactly. But what kind of parades did the people in Jesus' day know?

Well, the biggie was whenever the Roman ruler or Army would come to town, yesiree, that was a biggie. So everybody knew what the arrival of the King was like - or the arrival of the Emperor, or the arrival of God - for the Emperor *was* God. He came riding in with fanfare and his legions were dressed in fancy uniforms. He'd ride in on his war steed, a great huge, powerful horse that had been by his side through battle after battle where, of course, he'd been victorious. And they'd roll out the red carpet to show tribute and there'd be a huge stone arch - you can still find some of these statuary arches. All the wealthiest people would line the way which went through the best part of town. Of course, any riffraff would be shuttled out of sight. The homeless and the mentally ill, the street people - hustlers and prostitutes - might be rounded up and kept out of the way.

If you were poor in those days, you'd avoid that parade unless you could get a vantage point somewhere out of reach of the authorities.

And of course, everyone along the parade route would be cheering. That part hasn't changed, has it? We still cheer and hoorah when a particularly nice float or balloon goes by. Hosanna! Hoorah! Same thing.

So here comes Jesus into Jerusalem, just like one of the Roman rulers. Some folks in the crowd are even proclaiming him 'Messiah'! But there's differences too, aren't there? While it's like a parade of the Emperor, it's different too. Different in big ways!

First off, Jesus doesn't have legions of soldiers to clear the way, just two disciples. And he doesn't have a marvelous war steed, does he? No, just a donkey. Well, Matthew gives him a donkey and a colt but still - it's no war steed. It's just the basic animals of the common people. There's no 'victory' here, rather humility is the key element and Matthew ties this back to Zechariah, "Tell the daughter of Zion (which is Jerusalem), look, your king is coming to you, humble, and mounted on a donkey…" No, this is not a ruler like the people are familiar with, no sir.

And there's no tour through the best part of town, no, this parade goes right through the crowds. What does Matthew tell us? "A very large crowd." And did they roll out a red carpet? No - they spread their cloaks, the very cloaks off their backs, and branches from the trees, palm leaves just like the ones we have here this morning. Everybody was welcome at this parade! But boy, what a parade it must have been, what with everyone shouting and cheering the traditional Hebrew passover chants from Psalm 118, "Hosanna to the son of David! Blessed is the one who comes in the name of the Lord! Hosanna in the highest heaven! Why, they made such a ruckus, all these 'crowds', that "the whole city was in turmoil!" You see? This parade isn't just for the wealthy and privileged, it's for everyone in the whole city.

Hosanna! Hosanna in the highest heaven!

> [*pause*]

What would it have been like? Would we have been cheering like the crowds in the story? Or would we have been with the religious authorities and the Romans, rather outraged at this clear 'thumbing of the nose' to the Emperor? For that's another side to this parade - it's a parody of the triumphant entry by the Roman legions and Pontius Pilate. It's an 'in your face' gesture that certainly didn't sit well with the authorities.

But then, that's also part of the parabolic nature of this parade. You see, the kingdom of God is 'in your face' to all the powers and principalities! In God's kingdom, humility comes first - humility comes riding on a lowly donkey.

The kingdom of God is like a parade.

Hosanna! Hosanna in the highest heaven!

> [*pause*]

Here's another difference. In this parade, everyone's not only there, they all participate. 'The crowds went ahead of him and behind him', the text says. They didn't just stand there and wave as Jesus went by. They didn't just wave when given the high sign that he was coming. They didn't wait by the side of the road, no, they went ahead and behind, going right down the path with him! In Matthew's gospel, 'the crowds' is a general term meaning everyone, there's no separation by class or family or anything else that we know of. Like the way Jesus invites us to his meal, the Lord's Supper, he invites all.

Yes, the kingdom of God is like a parade.

Hosanna! Hosanna in the highest heaven!

[pause]

It's a parade alright - a wonderful, radical parade! In God's kingdom, the Lord is humble, sharing in the worldly trials of his sheep. In God's kingdom, all are welcome and invited to celebrate because justice comes first - the hungry are fed, the naked are clothed, the blind receive their sight, the lame walk! In God's kingdom, peace reigns and the powerful are brought low. Oh yes, the powers that be are brought low so they, too, can be part of the parade.

For you see, God's kingdom is - like a parade.

And that is good news, indeed! Amen.

Listen to the Cross
Psalm 22:1-2, 23-24

1 My God, my God, why have you forsaken me?
  Why are you so far from helping me, from the words of my groaning?
2 O my God, I cry by day, but you do not answer.
  and by night but find no rest.

23 You who fear the Lord, praise him!
  All you offspring of Jacob, glorify him.
  stand in awe of him, all you offspring of Israel!
24 For he did not despise or abhor
  the affliction of the afflicted.
he did not hide his face from me,
  but heard when I cried to him.

What does the cross mean to you? Is it a symbol of sacrificial atonement? A symbol of overwhelming love? Or maybe something else? So many points of view this afternoon - the centurions, the disciples, Pontius Pilate washing his hands. The cross speaks to us in many ways, doesn't it? I wonder - will we listen - to the cross?

  [*pause*]

Listening is hard, isn't it? I mean, it's different than just plain old hearing. Hearing requires little more than just recognizing that there's something audible going on. Hearing doesn't require that one actually pay attention. But listening is a different kettle of fish - the dictionary says, "'listen' - a verb, to make an effort to hear something, to pay attention, heed." Now, how many of you have children? Oh, well, see? I'm preaching to the experts here. You *know* that listening is different. You've all had to chase a kid around repeating furiously, "Listen to me! Listen to me! Listen to me!" We like to think this changes as we get older but, let's be honest, I don't want to count the times I've been listening to a friend at church only to realize they're waiting on my reply! I know I was hearing something, but listening? Not so much!

Yes, listening is different. You have to pay attention. You have to heed the message. Jesus says this a lot. The writers of Matthew, Mark and Luke all recount Jesus saying, "Let anyone with ears to hear - listen!" In one of my favorite passages where God speaks, even God says, "This is my son, the beloved, with whom I am well pleased, listen to him!" Listen!

Most of the time, we don't listen to the cross on Good Friday, we look at it. We see visual images of three crosses on a hill. Even the narratives about Good Friday are very visually driven. Take the gospel of Luke, for example. The whole narrative is full of 'show me' language. When Jesus is praying, it says, "in his anguish he prayed more earnestly, and his sweat became like great drops of blood falling down on the ground." And when he was arrested, "One of them struck the slave of the High Priest and cut off his right ear." And the writer of Mark tells us, "They clothed him in a purple cloak and, after twisting some thorns into a crown, they put it on him, they struck his head with a reed, spat upon him." And the final scene is an unforgettable image, "When it was noon, darkness came over the whole land until three in the afternoon." What imagery!

It's these visual images that show us the scene. Maybe we see ourselves standing in the crowd in Pilate's courtyard, screaming for Jesus to be crucified. Or maybe we see ourselves as one of the disciples - maybe Peter when he hears the cock crow for the third time. You know, Matthew tells us that Peter went out and wept bitterly. Can you see the tears running down his cheeks?

When we see that *we* put Jesus on the cross, we know a despair and a sense of sin that only Jesus can forgive - and then we know that Jesus died *for* us there on the cross.

   [*pause*]

But at the end, at the very moment of Jesus' death, it's not a video clip anymore, it's the audio track we hear. The writer of Matthew puts the words of Psalm 22:1-2 on Jesus' lips, telling us, "And about three o'clock Jesus cried with a loud voice, "My God, my God, why have you forsaken me?" But when we hear this, I think we can hear ourselves on the cross. We hear Jesus say - with us - as we, the psalmist, and Jesus cry out together, "My God, my God, why have you forsaken me?" And from there, we understand how Jesus dies *with* us, suffers *with* us on the cross. We know that feeling of being alone and we can see ourselves on our own crosses and we know that Jesus dies and suffers *with* us.

But we don't *listen* to the cross, do we? It's hard to listen. When I am judgmental, I'm not listening. When I am self-righteous, I'm not listening. Jesus made that clear for us in Matthew 25, verse 45, "Truly I tell you, just as you did not do it for one of the least of these, you did not do it for me." If we don't listen to each other, if we don't need each other, we're not listening to Jesus. We see the cross. We hear ourselves crying out from the cross, but we don't listen *to* the cross.

I tried to look for examples of our inability to listen - and I didn't have to look very far. One of the ones that came quickly to me, was pointed out so eloquently at Coretta Scott King's Memorial service just a few years ago. The outspoken Rev. Joseph Lowry, made it clear when he said, "For war, billions more - but no more for the poor." We don't listen very much to the poor. Funding to help deal with the HIV/AIDS pandemic was proposed and saw great announcements from our leaders. Yet quietly, these proposals are then cut from the budget. 25 million humans are crying out in Africa - most of them women and children - and we can't listen.

Let's look at the early part of the twentieth century. Lynchings were common, justified - even celebrated. Did you know that in 1921 down in Okemah, Oklahoma - Woody Guthrie's hometown - a black man was accused of stealing a sheep. When a deputy came to arrest him, the black man's 13-year-old son, not knowing what to do, scared and thinking the deputy' d already shot or drawn, shot the deputy with a 22 rifle. And the deputy bled to death in the yard. They arrested the black man, but later that week, a mob took the man's wife, the 13-year-old boy, and his baby brother - 16 months old - and hung them from the Canadian River bridge. Pictures were taken and later made into postcards and sold as souvenirs. Woody was always haunted by that postcard and years later he wrote a song. The chorus goes, "Don't kill my baby and my son! Don't kill my baby and my son! You can stretch my neck from that old river bridge, but don't kill my baby and my son!" People of color and minorities all around this country - and right here in Grand Island, NE - cry out - and we don't listen.

Let's talk about hunger. In the United States, 12 million children are hungry. In total, 36.3 million people in the United States are hungry. And yet hunger in the United States could be eliminated. Other countries, with the same average per capita income have done so. The hungry cry out - and we don't listen.

[*pause*]

Now, this could go on and on but it would just be self-flagellation because some of us do listen, at least a little. There are many programs ranging from local food pantries and shelters, to national relief efforts, to HIV/AIDS Awareness workshops. It's not that we don't *want* to listen or that we *don't* listen to Jesus - I think we're not listening - to the cross.

I'm going to shift gears briefly. I heard a wonderful story about Mother Teresa some years ago. A reporter was interviewing her and asked the question, "When you pray to God, what do you ask or say to God?" Mother Teresa quickly replied, "Oh, I don't speak - I just listen." The reporter, thinking quickly, asked, "Well, what does God say?" And again, Mother Teresa replied quickly, "Oh, God doesn't speak - God just listens." I like that! I like the idea of God listening with us, sharing in the paradox with us. David, in the Psalm today, starts out like this, he says he cries out but God does not answer. But even though David says God didn't answer - he says he heard. He says in verse 24, "He did not hide his face from me but heard when I cried to Him."

Just like God hears, God speaks too. Clearly, God spoke to Mother Teresa, telling her to help the poor all those years. Martin Luther King, Jr. heard God crying on behalf of people of color and all peoples living under oppression. And there are so many others that you could name for me if we had the time.

You see, God is talking to us. It's God crying out to us from Africa, from the hungry, from the 'least of these'. This is the third way to understand the cross today. It all gets back to listening to the cross. When we don't listen to each other, we're not listening to God; we're not listening to the cross. Oh sure, we look at the cross, we see Jesus, we see the Centurions, we see Jesus' mother and Mary weeping, but we don't listen! Who is it up there on the cross?

We find it so easy to listen to the one on the cross as though it's us but it isn't us. It's God. We *see* the body of Jesus but if we listen, we hear God crying out to us. God is on the cross! God incarnate in Jesus is crying out, "Why have you forsaken me?"

In a voice filled with all of our pain and suffering, rasping from all of our oppression and hate, in a voice filled with a love so overwhelming that even the sounds of the nails being pounded into the cross can't cover it up, we hear God! And then we know God loves us beyond death, beyond all time.

God cries out *for* us, *with* us, *to* us - hoping, hoping we'll listen - maybe a little bit. Maybe this time we'll listen - to the cross. Amen.

You Can't Keep A Good Man Down
Matthew 28:1-10

28 After the sabbath, as the first day of the week was dawning, Mary Magdalene and the other Mary went to see the tomb. 2 And suddenly there was a great earthquake; for an angel of the Lord, descending from heaven, came and rolled back the stone and sat on it. 3 His appearance was like lightning, and his clothing white as snow. 4 For fear of him the guards shook and became like dead men. 5 But the angel said to the women, "Do not be afraid; I know that you are looking for Jesus who was crucified. 6 He is not here; for he has been raised, as he said. Come, see the place where he[a] lay. 7 Then go quickly and tell his disciples, 'He has been raised from the dead, [b] and indeed he is going ahead of you to Galilee; there you will see him.' This is my message for you." 8 So they left the tomb quickly with fear and great joy and ran to tell his disciples. 9 Suddenly Jesus met them and said, "Greetings!" And they came to him, took hold of his feet, and worshiped him. 10 Then Jesus said to them, "Do not be afraid; go and tell my brothers to go to Galilee; there they will see me."

[This is a Reader's Theater-style play with the actors dispersed throughout the congregation. The Preacher or Worship Leader can play the role of the reporter]

Characters
Reporter: Inquisitive, empathetic.

Roman Guard: shocked, confused. Maybe a little irate; uncertain as to what actually occurred but convinced *something* happened!

Townsperson: fear, self-interest. 'I don't believe it', 'it'll get the authorities mad - this is not good'

Disciples: terror, disbelief with maybe. Denial - only speaking on condition of anonymity; surprise followed by... maybe - 'isn't this what he said would happen?' 'Where did Mary say he'd see us?'

Mary: amazement, love. Can't stop talking, overwhelmed - tells the story in a quick voice with lots of 'have I told you...' 'did I mention...?' and 'He greeted us - "chairo" he said.

Scene - Time and Place

We're in Jerusalem late morning after Jesus' tomb has been opened - broken into - in spite of Roman Guards watching over it - and Jesus is gone. There are claims of angels and even a sighting of Jesus alive.

~ ~ ~ ~ ~ ~ ~ ~ ~ ~ ~ ~ ~ ~ ~ ~

Reporter : This is Nathan Newman, your on-the-point reporter, coming to you live from Jerusalem with the big news of the day ! Some here in this Jewish town of Jerusalem are claiming that the radical, Jesus, who was crucified by the Romans just three days ago and buried, has been seen - alive! Certainly, it is a fact that the huge stone covering the tomb has been rolled away and the tomb is now empty. Who perpetrated this - and why - is not known at present but we hope to uncover some perspective this morning.

First, let's talk to one of the Guards who was actually there and witnessed this miraculous event.

[Move to the 'Roman Guard' Character]

Reporter : I'm here at the Imperial Palace of Pontius Pilate, the local Roman Authority. Several guards were assigned to keep watch over the Tomb of this radical, presumably to make sure something like this didn't happen - apparently, it wasn't enough!

Let's see if we can get a word with one of the guards. Sir - Sir, may we talk to you - were you there for the events at Jesus' tomb this morning?

Roman Guard: Yeah, I was there, what do you want to know?

Reporter : Well, what happened? Did you see Jesus or this angel we've heard rumors of? And, umm, didn't you crucify this Jesus a few days ago? Isn't it true that Roman crucifixion is usually fatal?

Roman Guard: Yes, he was crucified. Dead. There's no doubt about that! You want we should prove it - on you?

Reporter : No, no ! I'll take your word for it. But tell us about this morning...

Roman Guard: Well, nothing unusual had happened all night - we were expecting maybe his disciples might try to come and steal the body, but like I said, it was quiet. Until dawn, that's when [*hangs his head - almost in disbelief*] - something - happened. [*pause - then in a rush of words*] It seemed like the world was being torn apart! The ground started to shake and a deep rumble filled my head - it didn't come from anywhere in particular but it caught me so off-guard, I just stood there. Then lightning flashed and... and... well, I don't know exactly what it was - I could barely see after being blinded by the light - but something or somebody rolled that stone away! Whoever it was had to be powerful! It took five of us to roll it in place!

I don't know what happened after that. All I remember is finding myself getting water splashed on my face back here in the stables. And my so-called friends ribbing me - I don't care what they say - they weren't there. I don't know what it was, but I'm telling you - something happened - and it wasn't no crazy Jews robbing that tomb!

[*Reporter comes to center again*]

Reporter : Amazing. Well, let's see what some of the locals think about this.

[*moves to the 'Townsperson'*]

Reporter : Good morning, ma'am - can I have a word with you...?

Townsperson: Me? I didn't do nothin'... [*looks around, apprehensively*]

Reporter : Well no, I didn't say you did, I'd just like to get your take on this Jesus, this prophet some were saying was the King of the Jews. I'm sure you know he was crucified and buried recently but have you heard about what happened out at the tomb this morning?

Townsperson: That? Oh, that's got to be nonsense! Yeah, yeah - I heard about it, some wild story that an angel came and rolled the stone away and that Jesus is alive. I'm telling you, I ain't never seen nobody walk away from a crucifixion!

What do you want to be stirring this up for anyway? Haven't we got enough troubles without this? It's trouble from that no-good Jesus that got all this mess started! If you think the Romans were mad before, wait 'til this hits Pilate's fan! I'm gonna lay low, I am - and you'll do that too - if you know what's good for you. I'm tellin' you, the Romans won't like this - this is not good... [*sits, shaking her head, muttering to herself*]

[*Reporter comes to center again*]

Reporter : The news has spread, but it's not clear if it's good news...let's try to talk to a few of his disciples.

[*moves to the 'disciples'*]

Reporter : You - yes, both of you - can I ask you a few questions?

Disciple 1: What do you want to know?

Reporter : First, have you heard the news? That your leader, Jesus, has come back to life, has been resurrected and is no longer in the tomb?

Disciple 1: [*blinks several times, then whispers to his fellow disciple before answering*] Yeah - we heard - what's it to you?

Reporter : Well - aren't you excited? Don't you want to find him?

Disciple 1: [*looks around suspiciously*] Is this off the record? I'm not saying another word unless it's off the record...I'm anonymous, right?

Reporter : Yes, yes... go ahead...

Disciple 1: It's not right, it's not fair - he was tortured and brutally crucified - and now you want to get us out in the open with tales that he's resurrected - you'll just turn us in to Pilate and we'll be crucified too.

Disciple 2: [*talking to Disciple 1 rather than the reporter*] But wait - didn't he tell us this would happen? What if it's true John? What if he's - alive?

Disciple 1: [*replies to Disciple 2*] You think? Maybe we should find the others - did you hear where Mary said he'd see us...?

[*The disciples turn in private conversation; Reporter comes to center*]

Reporter : There's a report of several other eyewitnesses, let's see if we can find one of the Marys to talk to... [*move to 'Mary'*]

Reporter : Excuse me, miss, can I ask you some questions?

Mary: What? Ohh, isn't it glorious? Our Lord has risen! Praise God! Hosanna to the highest heaven! [*Reporter interrupts*]

Reporter: You saw it all, then?

Mary: Yes, yes, I saw it all! Praise God! We were going there - Mary and I - to see the tomb, we were so sad and missed him so. But then the ground shook and lightning flashed - the guards shook and fell dumb like statues. Did I tell you about the angel? An angel, oh, so brilliant! He rolled the stone away and light like I've never seen shone from inside the tomb. And Mary and I trembled, crying, and we were going to run away before the guards woke up and blamed us but the angel - did I tell you about the angel? The angel told us not to worry or be afraid. He said Jesus wasn't here anymore - he took us into the tomb and...and he was gone! All that was left was the shroud.

[*looks intently at the Reporter*] Are you one of our Lord's disciples? I don't remember you but if you are, the angel - did I mention the angel? oh yes, the angel said to go tell his disciples - have you seen any of them? We're still looking for them... [*look around as if looking for them...*]

Reporter: Did you actually see Jesus?

Mary: Yes, oh yes! Isn't it glorious? Our Lord has risen! Hosanna in the highest heaven!

Reporter: [*loses reporter's distance and becomes deeply involved, moved*] What did he say? Tell me - what did he say?

Mary: [*pause - remembering - beautiful smile, in a voice filled with awe*] He said, 'chairo' - greetings! After all he'd been through, he greeted us with joy and love. Can you believe it? [*laughs*] Chairo! We fell to our knees and worshipped at his feet and he told us to go and tell his brothers and sisters to go to Galilee - he'll see us all there. [*nodding head*]

Our Lord has risen! Chairo!

[*Reporter returns to center for last time*]

Reporter : There you have it. An amazing story - Jesus, who was crucified and died, has been resurrected! He's arisen! [*turn, pull out map and mutter, 'now, which way is it to Galilee?'*]

[*Preacher or Worship Leader can move to the pulpit or lectern to conclude the sermon*]

'Chairo' is the greek word that the resurrected Jesus first utters to the women. I am just taken aback, even now, 2 thousand years later, with the echo of that greeting! This word of greeting, a verb, especially so as a salutation, means be well - be glad, God speed, hail, joy, rejoice. How incongruous it must have seemed, the person who was crucified, greeting people. What kind of a love must you have to offer a warm, joyful greeting to the people who handed you over, who abandoned you, who forsook you even to death?

Do you know, the only other times this word appears in the New Testament is as a cynical torment? Judas says it right before giving Jesus that identifying kiss to hand him over to the authorities. And the Romans, after placing a crown of thorns roughly on his head, said it in cruel irony, "Chairo - Hail -, King of the Jews"

The resurrected Jesus comes to us even now, saying sincerely, "Chairo" - be well - be glad, God speed, hail, joy - rejoice!

And that is the best news ever! Amen!

The Price of Violence
Gen 6:9-22, 7:24, 8:14-19

9 These are the descendants of Noah. Noah was a righteous man, blameless in his generation; Noah walked with God. 10 And Noah had three sons, Shem, Ham, and Japheth. 11 Now the earth was corrupt in God's sight, and the earth was filled with violence. 12 And God saw that the earth was corrupt; for all flesh had corrupted its ways upon the earth. 13 And God said to Noah, "I have determined to make an end of all flesh, for the earth is filled with violence because of them; now I am going to destroy them along with the earth. 14 Make yourself an arc of cypress wood; make rooms in the ark and cover it inside and out with pitch. 15 This is how you are to make it: the length of the ark three hundred cubits, its width fifty cubits, and its height thirty cubits. 16 Make a roof for the ark and finish it to a cubit above; and put the door of the ark in its side; make it with lower, second, and third decks. 17 For my part, I am going to bring a flood of waters on the earth, to destroy from under heaven all flesh in which is the breath of life; everything that is on the earth shall die. 18 But I will establish my covenant with you; and you shall come into the ark, you, your sons, your wife, and your sons' wives with you. 19 And of every living thing, of all flesh, you shall bring two of every kind into the ark, to keep them alive with you; they shall be male and female. 20 Of the birds according to their kinds, and of the animals according to their kinds, of every creeping thing of the ground according to its kind, two of every kind shall come into you, to keep them alive. 21 Also take with you every kind of food that is eaten and store it up; and it shall serve as food for you and for them." 22 Noah did this; he did all that God commanded him.

24 And the waters swelled on the earth for one hundred fifty days.

14 In the second month, on the twenty-seventh day of the month, the earth was dry. 15 Then God said to Noah, 16 "Go out of the ark, you and your wife, and your sons and your sons' wives with you. 17 Bring out with you every living thing that is with you of all flesh—birds and animals and every creeping thing that creeps on the earth—so that they may abound on the earth, and be fruitful and multiply on the earth." 18 So Noah went out with his sons and his wife and his sons' wives. 19 And every animal, every creeping thing, and every bird, everything that moves on the earth, went out of the ark by families.

Today, we're beginning our summer-long exploration into some of the great stories in the Old Testament or Hebrew Bible. Yes, scholars today prefer to use the term 'Hebrew Bible' for those books from Genesis all the way to Malachi. Of course, we're not going to plow through all of this in just one summer! No, actually, we're only going to get into the Pentateuch - the first five books of the Hebrew Bible and, to be totally accurate, we're actually only going to make it partway into Exodus!

You know, we could also refer to the Hebrew Bible as Jesus' Bible - since it was - Jesus was very familiar with it, as was any good Jew of his time. So we're going to be reading in the books of Genesis and Exodus; these are in the section or books known as the 'primeval or primary history'. These are narratives - they are best understood by their identity as whole stories rather than as isolated pieces. The HarperCollins Bible Commentary says, "It would be more appropriate to understand them - even the Ten Commandments - not as laws claiming universal truth, but as texts that will yield meanings only as they are understood within the narrative framework that surrounds them." I recommend this commentary to you - it's got a lot of good background information about the Hebrew Bible in general.

So we're going to be reading along in Genesis and Exodus about the Patriarchs of the faith - Noah, Abram/Abraham, Isaac, Jacob, Joseph, Moses. But as the old saying goes, "Behind every great man is an amazing woman," so we'll not forget about Sarai/Sarah, Hagar, Rebekah, Zipporah. In fact, they're some of the best characters in these narratives! But I digress - enough background Bible study stuff. Let's get back to our story for this week, the story of the flood and Noah and God's first covenant with us.

[*pause*]

First of all, this is a scary story, isn't it? I mean, wiping out everything? Total wipe out? It's like, well, it's like going right back to the beginning, isn't it? In the broadest sense, this story is a contrast with Genesis 1 taking us back to the chaos before creation. It's like God was drawing out the story of history, got to this point and [*crumple up paper and toss it over shoulder to start again*] ... or maybe it's the shaking up of a great cosmic etch-a-sketch. Any way you look at it though, it's a new beginning.

What is it that brings God to this point? What is it that is so upsetting to God that God would even consider such a drastic turn of events?

Violence. "Now the earth was corrupt in God's *sight*, and the earth was filled with violence." Contrast this to Genesis 1:31a: "God *saw* everything that he had made, and, indeed, it was very good." What happened? Well, some might say Adam and Eve's disobedience was the start of all this but that was also a fall upwards in that we did get knowledge - and God didn't kill Adam and Eve. I think if you go back just a few verses to 6:5, there's another version: "The LORD saw that the wickedness of humankind was great in the earth, and that every inclination of the thoughts of their hearts was only evil continually."

[step aside; pause]

Now, we could get into a lovely discussion of how there are two flood narratives here, two versions. One version refers to God as "God" while the other to God as "YHWH" which is shown in the text as LORD all in caps. There's also the little problem that one version says the water came for 'forty days and forty nights' while ours today says "the waters swelled on the earth for one hundred fifty days."

But that would be more Bible study and I'm not going to talk about that today.

No, I want to stick to the whole issue of violence. Does anyone else besides me conclude that God really doesn't like violence?! I mean really, really abhors violence. You simply can't miss that in this narrative. And I can't help but see a comparison or contrast with the wars in Iraq and Afghanistan. Or the violence in Darfur and other places in Africa or the violence - well - all over the world!

Somehow, we convince ourselves that there's something right and proper about *fighting* for justice, for freedom. We create an illusion for ourselves that violence is okay if it's for those reasons. We create for ourselves an illusion of freedom but who's kidding who? What sort of freedom is it that needs to be maintained with violence? How 'free' is that? *[shake my head]*

If I had more time, I might talk about that - but I'm not going to talk about that today.

No, what I really want to talk about is another side of violence. There are those obvious sorts of physical violence, that's easy to see and understand. Biblically, it starts with Cain and Abel and God doesn't like that at all. When God finds out, God cries out, "What have you done? Listen: your brother's blood is crying out to me from the ground!" That's physical violence that God doesn't like.

But there are more subtle forms of violence, too, aren't there? There's the violence of prejudice and hatred. There's the violence of racism and any other kind of 'ism' that puts one person above another. There's the violence of bullying. There's the violence we perpetrate on each other in the name of judgment. Of course, that one can be balanced out with a well-placed 'bless their heart!' But maybe that's just another illusion, too; the illusion that by a simple 'bless their heart' we've offset the violence. Probably not, huh?!

I heard a story about a little church a long time ago - maybe it was when Nebraska was a frontier state. Anyway, it seems one Sunday a newcomer to the town showed up at church for Sunday worship, dressed all casual-like. Now mind you, this was way before our 'casual Friday' dress codes. He had on dirty jeans, a work shirt with a torn sleeve, and boots that clearly hadn't ever been polished. Everybody looked rather askance at him, clearly judging him to be inappropriate in the Lord's House. After the service, the minister greeted him, thanked him for coming but then said, "Maybe this week, you should have a talk with God about what you should wear when you come to church on Sunday." You know, 'helping' him to see the error of his ways.

Next Sunday comes around - and there he is again. And once again, he's dressed in his dirty jeans, torn shirt and old boots. If anything, everyone's disdain was even worse. This morning, at the end of the service, the minister's greeting was a little chillier. He said, "Glad to see you again but, ohh, didn't you have that talk with God?"

The visiting stranger answered, "Why yessir, I did. But God said he's never been here so he wasn't exactly sure what I should wear."

[*pause*]

You see? Our violence can be as subtle as a well-intentioned word of advice that never was asked for in the first place. It can be a thoughtless gesture never meant to harm but no less violent for all that.

There's a story I've seen several times on the internet. A boy, Tommy maybe, walking home from school, sees some kids trip another kid, knocking him to the ground sending his books everywhere. When he gets to the kid, he sees it's the loner, the kid who always seemed shy and quiet. He lives in the neighborhood but Tommy never really knew him. Tommy was going to just walk on by but, for some reason, stopped and helped the kid. And then walked home with him, just talking, just being friendly.

Several years later, both boys were graduating and the one who'd fallen turned out to be class valedictorian. He said he wanted to thank Tommy, the boy who stopped, that he was responsible for him even graduating. You see, that day long ago, when the other kids tripped him, had been the final straw. He'd made his mind up to go home and kill himself. But Tommy, who came along, helped him, walked with him - changed everything.

[*pause*]

But I don't want to talk about that, not even about that subtle violence.

No, what I really want to talk about is - Noah. What makes him so special? Why does he get the 'Ark Franchise', so to speak? The text we read says, "Noah was a righteous man, blameless in his generation;" Okay, so he's a good guy. But it's the very next line that spoke to me this week: "Noah walked with God."

"Noah walked with God."

Do you walk with God? What does it mean to walk with God? Well, I think it means all the obvious things - things like praying, being nice when you should, maybe putting some change in the Salvation Army bucket each Christmas, coming to worship each Sunday, faithfully supporting the church and our ministry. But I think it means much more than that too. I think it means becoming more aware of all the forms of violence we participate in. It means not being so judgmental, maybe not getting so angry when driving just because there's people who drive badly - bless their hearts...

It means beginning to look past our illusions, the ways we rationalize and convince ourselves that what we're doing is not so bad - it's all in a good cause, after all.

It means trusting God to be God. It means giving up our tendency to 'help God out'. It means letting go of our shoulds and oughts.

It means letting go of the violence that keeps us away from God. You see, that's the real price of violence. When we're violent, we're not walking with God. It's not possible to be violent and walk with God. That's the real cost. How much is having your own way worth? Is it worth giving up your walk with God just to feel self-righteously right and justified? Is it worth being violent if that's what it costs?

One young boy didn't think so - and he saved a life because he chose not to be violent like the other kids. Noah didn't think so - and he got the franchise for the biggest Ark project in the history of the world!

Noah walked with God - and because of that - so can we. Yeah, that's what I really wanted to talk about today.

For that is truly good news! Amen.

Promises Kept
Genesis 21:1-7

21 The Lord dealt with Sarah as he had said, and the Lord did for Sarah as he had promised. 2 Sarah conceived and bore Abraham a son in his old age, at the time of which God had spoken to him. 3 Abraham gave the name Isaac to his son whom Sarah bore him. 4 And Abraham circumcised his son Isaac when he was eight days old, as God had commanded him. 5 Abraham was a hundred years old when his son Isaac was born to him. 6 Now Sarah said, "God has brought laughter for me; everyone who hears will laugh with me." 7 And she said, "Who would ever have said to Abraham that Sarah would nurse children? Yet I have borne him a son in his old age."

This saga, from the primeval history about our archetypal forefathers, Abraham and Sarah, is a long, rambling account of a human family - with all its foibles and warts there for all to see! It actually began back in chapter 12 with Abram's call. Today, we're looking at the birth of Isaac, Abraham and Sarah's son and certainly, the very first verse says it all: "The LORD dealt with Sarah as he had said, and the LORD did for Sarah as he had promised."

Wait a second - last week, wasn't 'the promise' made to Abram? And when did Sarai's name change? Yeah, a lot has happened to Abram and Sarai between our first hearing of them in chapter 12 and now here in chapter 21! And actually, Abraham and Sarah's story goes on all the way to Chapter 25. So let's see - Genesis has - how many chapters? That's right - 50. And the Abraham/Sarah sequence is 14 chapters long. That's over 1/4th of the whole book! The Jacob saga and the Joseph saga only have 12 chapters each. In fact, Abraham/Sarah, Jacob, and Joseph make up 3/4th of the whole book of Genesis. Our entire history is based on a bunch of wild characters! And family values? Well, family values are all well and good but I'm not sure we want to hold onto some of these 'family values!'

Abraham sets the family tone by pimping his wife - not once, but twice! - so he'll save his own skin. Then Jacob hoodwinks the family birthright from his older brother, Esau. Finally, Joseph's brothers sell him off into Egypt and he runs them in circles before reuniting the family! And let's not even think about all the kids' actual parentage. No, while we can learn much from Genesis, 'family values' have changed way too much since ancient times!

But I'm drifting here - where were we? Oh yes - we're with Abraham and Sarah. Well, before we can understand our text today, we'd better go back and touch at least some of the earlier sections of the story. "The LORD dealt with Sarah as he had said..." Where did YHWH speak to Sarah? Well, it's back in the great hospitality story in chapter 18. After Abraham has offered hospitality to the strangers, "They said to him, "Where is your wife Sarah?" And he said, "There, in the tent." Then one said, "I will surely return to you in due season, and your wife Sarah shall have a son." And Sarah was listening at the tent entrance behind him. Now Abraham and Sarah were old, advanced in age; it had ceased to be with Sarah after the manner of women. So Sarah laughed to herself, saying, "After I have grown old, and my husband is old, shall I have pleasure?" The LORD said to Abraham, "Why did Sarah laugh, and say, 'Shall I indeed bear a child, now that I am old? Is anything too wonderful for the LORD? At the set time I will return to you, in due season, and Sarah shall have a son." But Sarah denied, saying, "I did not laugh"; for she was afraid. God said, "Oh yes, you did laugh."

See? That's what our text today is referring to - God promised Abraham and Sarah that they'd have a son. Of course, it really goes all the way back to the promise God made to Abram in last week's text: "I will make of you a great nation, and I will bless you..."

So God's made this promise to Abram and Sarai, this outlandish promise that they'll be blessed with a huge family. This impossible promise that old, infertile Sarah will have a son.

And it happens!

"Now Sarah said, "God has brought laughter for me; everyone who hears will laugh with me." And she said, "Who would ever have said to Abraham that Sarah would nurse children? Yet I have borne him a son in his old age."

This huge story, seemingly revolving around Sarah, really is about God. God makes a promise. Sarai doesn't believe it. She's barren, so first, she has her slave woman, Hagar, have a child with Abram. Then she gets angry with her and sends her away. Then, after God says she'll still have children, she laughs at God! As an aside, check the other version of this story in chapter 17 and see who's laughing.

[pause]

Have you ever made a promise to someone - and they laughed at you? Or maybe someone made a promise to you and it was so outlandish, before you could stop yourself, you laughed at them? We all do this, you know. Ohh, maybe most of us only do it when we're younger, you know, the sort of things kids says, "I'm going to be president someday." I wonder if John McCain or

Barack Obama said that when they were kids? If they did, it looks like one of them is going to keep that promise this fall.

I once said I'd win the Nobel prize someday! Go ahead, you can laugh - it's not gonna happen. I also thought I'd write a book someday - now I suppose that could still happen. And I know I said I'd record an album of music someday - and now I have four but I'm pretty sure somebody at least chuckled whenever I said these promise statements.

These are just human promises, we all know those can slip through our fingers. What about God's promises? Will God keep God's promises - to us?

[*pause*]

It reminds me of the story of Yeshua and the Yoomba tree. Now Yeshua grew up not far from here, just over the second set of hills on the north side of St. Paul. Well, where St. Paul is now - this was a long time ago! Yeshua's family was part of the buffalo clan; they usually migrated with the herds across these wide-open grasslands. But her family had settled in the hills around the Loup river valley and there they were when Yeshua came into this world.

Yeshua's mother and father were old. They were so old, no one could actually remember when they came to this valley. They were so old; they were almost grandparents before they ever had Yeshua! But, ohh, they were so surprised when Yeshua came along. And so happy for they didn't have any other children - just little Yeshua, their beloved daughter. But being an only child was hard for little Yeshua. Her family had settled - along with the others from her clan - because they were too old to follow the herds anymore. There were a few other children but they were all older than Yeshua so she mostly had to entertain herself. So it wasn't at all surprising to find her playing down by the Yoomba tree.

Now the Yoomba tree - you do know what a Yoomba tree is, don't you? - you don't? Well, they are one of the most amazing trees you could ever see. It's a sort of a cross between the Caribbean Banyan tree and a weeping willow tree. It's big and round with lots of crooked roots to leave plenty of good seats for a little girl and all her imaginary friends. And it has the very best shade the way the tops of the limbs spread out like a willow tree. But probably the biggest difference between the Yoomba tree and all the other trees were the long bean-like seed pods that hung down on slender threads each spring and sometimes even into the summer. The Yoomba tree has another unusual trait too.

When those long, stringbean-like pods ripen, they burst with a loud pop and seeds almost like the cottonwood tree explode out and drift on the breeze. That was probably one of the things Yeshua liked about the Yoomba tree the best. She and Marciann and Benjmin - they're her friends that only she can see - loved to go down to the Yoomba tree and listen as the pods snapped open. They'd all laugh and dance under the swaying branches.

Now sometimes, when Yeshua would go there by herself, she'd talk to the Creator, to God, just sure that God liked the Yoomba tree as much as she did. When Yeshua was sad, she could always share it with God. In fact, she often told God how she wished she had some other children to play with, some friends she could laugh with there under the Yoomba tree. And do you know what? God spoke to Yeshua there under the Yoomba tree with the sunlight leaking through the leaves.

God said, "Yeshua, when you get older, I promise that you will be a delight to all children just as you have been a delight to my friend, the Yoomba tree." You see, God did like the Yoomba tree, almost as much as Yeshua did!

So time passed; Yeshua grew into a teenager and didn't visit the Yoomba tree as much. But in the springtime, she'd still go when the seed pods were blossuming and she'd laugh as they'd pop and scatter their seeds. Then she got even older and left for her life as an adult. Yeshua went away to the big city, to Lincoln where she went to school and studied to be a teacher. And she became a wonderful teacher. Of course she was good with kids. Somehow, she always remembered God's promise to her under the Yoomba tree, that she'd be a delight to children. But she always thought that they'd be her own children. Sadly, that wasn't to be. Yeshua lived alone all her life.

When her parents died, she moved back to the clan homestead. It was a small, almost empty village by then. Yeshua didn't know what to do - but she knew how to teach. So she started a small school to teach the children who were slowly moving into the region. Eventually, she had to move to a bigger schoolhouse as her classes grew. But no matter how big her class grew; she took them every spring to the Yoomba tree. Yes, the Yoomba tree was still there! And her children - for that's the way she thought of them by then - would all smile and laugh as she laughed each time one of the Yoomba tree seed pods would pop open. Do you know, I think even the Yoomba tree smiled - if a Yoomba tree could smile?

But life must move on as it does for us all and, in the proper time, Yeshua died peacefully. At her request, her ashes were scattered there around the Yoomba tree, just over the second set of hills on the north side of St. Paul.

You know, the children still go play around the Yoomba tree in the springtime. The last time I was there, they told me that you could still hear Yeshua laughing each time a seed pod popped open. The gentle ring of her laughter seems to spill out and follow the seeds as the limbs of the graceful tree wave them onward to the delight of children everywhere and always.

Promises kept. A child is born - children laugh in delight. Promises kept.

   [*pause*]

What about Jesus' promises? We heard one of those not too long ago, just back in the middle of May, the very last verse in the gospel of Matthew: "And remember, I am with you always, to the end of the age." Is this a real, honest-to-God, promise like the promise YHWH gave Abraham and Sarah, like the promise God gave Yeshua?

I think it is. I really do.

And that is such good news! Amen.

An Impossible Request
Genesis 22:1-14

22 After these things God tested Abraham. He said to him, "Abraham!" And he said, "Here I am." 2 He said, "Take your son, your only son Isaac, whom you love, and go to the land of Moriah, and offer him there as a burnt offering on one of the mountains that I shall show you." 3 So Abraham rose early in the morning, saddled his donkey, and took two of his young men with him, and his son Isaac; he cut the wood for the burnt offering, and set out and went to the place in the distance that God had shown him. 4 On the third day Abraham looked up and saw the place far away. 5 Then Abraham said to his young men, "Stay here with the donkey; the boy and I will go over there; we will worship, and then we will come back to you." 6 Abraham took the wood of the burnt offering and laid it on his son Isaac, and he himself carried the fire and the knife. So the two of them walked on together. 7 Isaac said to his father Abraham, "Father!" And he said, "Here I am, my son." He said, "The fire and the wood are here, but where is the lamb for a burnt offering?" 8 Abraham said, "God himself will provide the lamb for a burnt offering, my son." So the two of them walked on together.

9 When they came to the place that God had shown him, Abraham built an altar there and laid the wood in order. He bound his son Isaac, and laid him on the altar, on top of the wood. 10 Then Abraham reached out his hand and took the knife to kill his son. 11 But the angel of the Lord called to him from heaven, and said, "Abraham, Abraham!" And he said, "Here I am." 12 He said, "Do not lay your hand on the boy or do anything to him; for now I know that you fear God, since you have not withheld your son, your only son, from me." 13 And Abraham looked up and saw a ram, caught in a thicket by its horns. Abraham went and took the ram and offered it up as a burnt offering instead of his son. 14 So Abraham called that place "The Lord will provide"; as it is said to this day, "On the mount of the Lord it shall be provided."

Do you find this story about Abraham and Isaac troublesome? Yeah, me too. In the past few weeks, I have been trying for the life of me to figure out what to say about it! There's an awful lot going on in this short story and I could easily spend all my time just talking about the details and the underlying cultural and social mores that are implicit in it, such as sacrifice. We'll have to talk about that a great deal for that is at the heart of this tale. We'll also have to talk about the problematic way "God" says one thing then seemingly changes "God's" mind. We'll have to figure out whether this says anything about "God" or actually says much more about us and the way we tend to make God in *our* image.

You know what I mean. The delightful authoress, Anne Lamott, in one of her books - I can't recall which - tells of an alcoholic priest friend of hers who summed this up rather succinctly when he advised her that, "You can be pretty sure you've made God in your image when God hates the same people you do."

That gets at the real heart of this - what is it God expects of us? What can we do that will please God? To get us started, let's just look closer at the story. There's some crucial things to notice right off the bat. First, in the very first verse, the Hebrew word translated simply as "God" is ha'Elohim - it's a priestly term for God - literally - 'the God'. And it is 'the God' that tells Abraham to sacrifice Isaac. And, apparently, Abraham goes right ahead with this grisly request made all the more awful by the detail, "Take your son, your only son, whom you love..." There's no way to miss that this request isn't just for a little commitment here, this isn't a polite request of a little support, no, this is maximum sacrifice, awful, terrible sacrifice of the most precious thing to Abraham.

Can you even imagine being asked to make such a sacrifice?

The next part of the story is where I really begin to question just what's going on. It says, "So Abraham rose early in the morning..." Wait a second - what happened to Abraham? This isn't the 'Abraham" who just last week was "very distressed on account of his son." Oh...maybe there's a parallel going on here. In last week's story, - in Genesis 21:8-21, Sarah essentially asks Abraham to kill his son Ishmael. Now, he's been asked to sacrifice his promised son, Isaac, the promise of the covenant. And, indeed, the words are the same in last week's story, "So Abraham rose early in the morning..." But then, in the Ishmael story, YHWH tells Abraham not to worry....

[*pause*]

So the element of sacrifice is common to both these stories and they are very carefully woven so that the listener sees the parallel. So I guess we can't avoid it - we'll have to talk about sacrifice. And I apologize right now - this part is gruesome, there's no way around it if we want to come to grips with this gruesome story.

In ancient religious cults, sacrifice was a common thing. It was an offering to God or the Gods. One of the most ancient and common forms was the offering of first fruits of animals and vegetables. King and Stager, in *Life in Biblical Israel*, point out "Their purpose was to acknowledge that the land and its produce belonged to God as creator. The first fruits were considered the best yield of the harvest. Such offerings symbolized the donor's gratitude to and dependence upon YHWH; at the same time, they were considered a guarantee of future productivity."[1]

And in Israelite religious practice, "first fruits" includes the firstborn - of everything - animals and children. Exodus 22:29b - "The firstborn of your sons you shall give to me." However, the Levites were accepted as a group to substitute for the firstborn of all the Israelites: Numbers 3:11-13a - "Then YHWH spoke to Moses, saying: 'I hereby accept the Levites from among the Israelites as substitutes for all the firstborn that open the womb among the Israelites. The Levites shall be mine, for all the firstborn are mine...'" King and Stager go on to clarify, "It may be that the firstborn was originally not meant to be sacrificed but were to serve in the role of priests before the priesthood was established."[2]

However, such human sacrifice was practiced. This is very, very difficult for us to even grasp, but it's important to begin to recognize the way we can transfer our thoughts onto God and then trick ourselves into believing they're what God wants. If you buy into the sacrificial system and say, okay, God wants the first fruits, you can literally follow that right along logically into God wants my firstborn offered up in a burnt offering.

Our text today is the crucial turning point. YHWH God steps in at the crucial point and says no, don't kill your child, your faithfulness is what I want. Did you catch that? The word for God changed - it's not 'the God', now it's YHWH. The Israelites would never have missed the change in name from Elohim to YHWH. There's an implicit lean towards YHWH, Israel's God, not desiring child sacrifice.

Whew! We can breathe a sigh of relief! God does not expect us to offer our firstborn as a burnt offering! Yet they did it. In the Bible, two kings of Judah are attested to have offered their sons and daughters as human sacrifices, Ahaz and Manasseh in 2 Kings 16 and 21. But the prophet Jeremiah rails against this in 7:30-31: "For the people of Judah have done evil in my sight, says YHWH; they have set their abominations in the house that is called by my name, defiling it. And they go on building the high place of Tophet, which is in the valley of the son of Hinnom, to burn their sons and their daughters in the fire - which I did not command, nor did it come into my mind."

If it didn't come into YHWH's mind, whose idea was it?

[pause]

Let's take a deep breath and go back to our story before we circle back to this whole question of sacrifice and what God expects of us, okay? There's still this issue of Abraham just going right ahead with this request. My first gut reaction whenever I read this story is to get mad at Abraham. I want to shake him and tell him, "Say no! Say no, I won't kill my son!" And I think that's what Abraham - at least, the Abraham I see in the earlier stories, would say. I mean, where's the Abraham who bargains with YHWH for the righteous in Sodom and Gomorrah? The Abraham who says in Genesis 18 - "Will you indeed sweep away the righteous with the wicked? Suppose there are fifty righteous within the city, will you then sweep away the place and not forgive it for the fifty righteous who are in it? Far be it from you to do such a thing, to slay the righteous with the wicked." God says, okay, I'll forgive the whole place for their sake, but Abraham isn't done. He says, "Let me take upon myself to speak to the Lord, I who am but dust and ashes..." He keeps bargaining until he's got YHWH to agree that even if there are just 10 righteous men, he'll forgive the whole city.

Where's this Abraham? I want him in this story about Isaac! Where's the Abraham who slyly tells his wife to pretend to be his sister so he won't get killed? Where's the Abraham who's so distressed by Sarah's request that he sentence Ishmael to death?

You see? We're being setup in this story. We're being setup to feel the incredible tension of such an impossible request. We're being forced to examine what we'd do - we can't count on Father Abraham to help us out. Actually, I think the tension keeps us from seeing the fact that in the story last week, YHWH tells Abraham YHWH won't let Ishmael die. It keeps us from noticing Abraham's unconscious slip when he tells his workers that he *and the boy* will return after they worship, his slip that he tells Isaac that God will provide the lamb. I'll tell you what I think - I think Abraham was in on the deal, I think we've been setup by Abraham in this story to make sure we question what we'd do for God.

Will we get caught up in worship practices thinking that's what God wants? Will we create God in *our* image so we can accept bad behavior and selfishness and literal atrocities because 'God wants us to do it'?

What does God want us to do anyway? See? I told you we'd circle back to this. The prophets have a lot to say about this, about the way the people substituted their ideas in place of God's ideas. Listen to Isaiah in chapter 58: "Is not this the fast that I choose: to loose the bonds of injustice, to undo the thongs of the yoke, to let the oppressed go free, and to break every yoke? Is it not to share your bread with the hungry, and bring the homeless poor into your house; when you see the naked, to cover them, and not to hide yourself from your own kin?"

The prophet Micah brings this whole question into direct light: "With what shall I come before YHWH, and bow myself before God on high? Shall I come before him with burnt offerings, with calves a year old? Will YHWH be pleased with thousands of rams, with ten thousand of rivers of oil? Shall I give my firstborn for my transgression, the fruit of my body for my sins? He has showed you, O mankind, what is good; and what does YHWH require of you but to do justice, and to love kindness, and to walk humbly with your God?" (Micah 6:6-8)

Do you think maybe all Abraham was doing was walking humbly with his God, YHWH? Trusting that YHWH would, indeed, provide? You know what I think? I think Abraham never would've actually done it, I think even with the knife raised, he would've said, "No! *The* God that asks such a terrible thing of me is not *my* God!" I think Abraham would've recognized that 'the God' was much more a God made in our image than the ultimate unknowable mystery that *is* YHWH God.

Here's what else I think - when I think 'God' is telling me that I'm better than someone else and so it's okay to put them down in harsh judgement, I need to say no to that 'God'. I think when my 'God' says my religion, my denomination, is better than everyone else's, I need to turn my back on that 'God'. When 'the God' says it's okay for me to keep more of my money and time just because I think I've done something especially good, I need to run from that idolatrous 'God' created in my image!

Ultimate mystery, father and mother of all that is, creator - YHWH - what do you expect of me? To do justice, to love kindness, and to walk humbly with your God. What do you think, did Jesus get the essence of that when he told us his commandment - "love one another, as I have loved you?"

We're the ones who make impossible requests; whatever God asks of us is possible - for YHWH will provide.

And that is good news! Amen.

---

[1] Philip J. King and Lawrence E. Stager Life *in Biblical Israel*, (Westminster John Knox Press: Louisville, KY), 2001, p. 358.

[2] Ibid., p. 359.

Thin Spaces
Genesis 28:10-19a

10 Jacob left Beer-sheba and went toward Haran. 11 He came to a certain place and stayed there for the night, because the sun had set. Taking one of the stones of the place, he put it under his head and lay down in that place. 12 And he dreamed that there was a ladder set up on the earth, the top of it reaching to heaven; and the angels of God were ascending and descending on it. 13 And the Lord stood beside him and said, "I am the Lord, the God of Abraham your father and the God of Isaac; the land on which you lie I will give to you and to your offspring; 14 and your offspring shall be like the dust of the earth, and you shall spread abroad to the west and to the east and to the north and to the south; and all the families of the earth shall be blessed in you and in your offspring. 15 Know that I am with you and will keep you wherever you go, and will bring you back to this land; for I will not leave you until I have done what I have promised you." 16 Then Jacob woke from his sleep and said, "Surely the Lord is in this place—and I did not know it!" 17 And he was afraid, and said, "How awesome is this place! This is none other than the house of God, and this is the gate of heaven."

18 So Jacob rose early in the morning, and he took the stone that he had put under his head and set it up for a pillar and poured oil on the top of it. 19 He called that place Bethel; but the name of the city was Luz at the first.

Did you catch the title to this morning's sermon - "Thin Spaces 2"? Yes, I'm afraid sermons are getting to be like the movies - you get a good one and they make a sequel out of it! Sort of like Shrek 2 or Toy Story 2. You know the sequel is going to follow similar story lines and some of the characters will be the same, the ones who'll have the biggest draw at the box office, I guess. But wasn't the original one good - "Thin Spaces Between Earth and God"? What? You don't remember it?! [*grin*]

Well, it was way back on June 8th and the text was the opening text in the Abraham/Sarah sequence, Genesis 12:1-9 - let's hear them again. [*read Genesis 12:1-9*]

So if that was the original, this story of Jacob is clearly the sequel, 'Thin Spaces 2'. In the original, there were just two characters - a human and YHWH: in the sequel, there's a human and YHWH. In the original, the human is amazed by his encounter with God - same in the sequel. In the original, the human marks the spot with an altar - same in the sequel. Here's what I said back then: When God speaks to Abram, this is like a whisper, not a shout: it's a 'thin space' - the place where the distance between us and God gets thin. When we're at the 'thin space' - as scary as that may be - we find God. And I talked about some examples, places where I felt a 'thin space', where I felt close to God: like being called to be a counselor at Kamp Kaleo, Marcella's return to worship.

I had another one not too long ago - I was on retreat at St. Scholastica Monastery in Fort Smith, AR. As part of my meditative practice, I sometimes like to get up early enough to watch the sunrise. I left the dormitory in the dark and found a comfortable place to watch the eastern sky for the breaking of the day. Dawn crept forward - and so did the clouds! Frustrated and impatient, I moved to the Labyrinth and began to walk it. I'd walk a few minutes then stop and look for the sun. Walk a bit more and look again.

As it turned out, at each corner outside the Labyrinth, there were small flower beds. After walking and looking for the sun and walking some more, I finally noticed a nice daisy in the flower bed. It, too, was waiting, looking east, for the sun. And it was doing it with much more patience than I! Such are the thin spaces all around us.

Of course, at thin spaces, you have to do something - there's no option to do nothing when it comes to 'thin spaces' - doing nothing is a choice to turn away, to not respond to God, to stay in our world, illusory as that may be. If you avoid the 'thin spaces' you might stay safe - but you'll miss the blessings. When you respond to the 'thin spaces', God appears to you; when you respond to the 'thin spaces', you get to praise God in thankful prayer. When you respond, a simple daisy can teach you about profound mystery.

[*pause*]

So, what if you do nothing? What if Jacob had awoken, shook his head and said, "Wow. I sure had a weird dream last night - must've been that camel stew I had for supper." What if he'd just blown it off, would he have taken any special note of it? Would he have built an altar to mark the place? Would he have recognized God's presence in that place? Would he have seen it as 'the gate of heaven'?

Would you?

What if you had a dream, a vision, a message that, for just a fleeting instant, seemed to be God's presence right - next - to - you? Would you recognize it? Or would it simply be something you ate or maybe just a stupid flower or stupid clouds? The Franciscan priest, Murray Bodo, would recognize it; he echoes my feelings in his book of poetry and meditation, *Song of the Sparrow* so well, I'm paraphrasing liberally from it here:

"Our lives are a forgetting and remembering, a rhythm that follows us relentlessly till death. Mostly, we're alive and busy 'doing', and we try to forget the fears and anxieties we feel about the future - they paralyze us in the present and make us dead and inactive. We are people who hope and believe, so we try to remember the good that God has done for us. And when we recall God's faithfulness and care, we become men and women of the future who dare to act because we forget our failures and remember God's action in our every thought and deed. We stay sane because our eyes are on God who loves us and proves it when we dare to live for God. Then, we notice the thin spaces. If we remember to *remember* God, we find our lives are meaningful and free."[1]

Of course, the 'thin spaces' are God's, "you can't merit such an experience. Yet, we still long for God to speak or reveal that God is there. Is this selfishness? No, I don't think it is because this longing is something beyond our control. Turn wherever we may, nothing and no one short of God can satisfy our longing or distract us from that gnawing in our minds and hearts which speaks of an emptiness yet to be filled.

All of us who turn to God, at one time or another, ask if God really exists. And maybe we wonder if we're only deceiving ourselves in order to give meaning to our own unfulfilled lives? But then subtly, in ways we did not expect, God comes to us fleetingly - in the 'thin spaces' - to keep alive the longing and the hope of the resurrected life to come. God never comes on our terms but in God's own time and place; it's a surprise! No one ever sees God, of course, but we see the shadows of God's passing through our lives in the things that change which we thought never would - in the prayers that are answered in ways that we never expected - in a new level of maturity that we know we couldn't have arrived at alone. And once again, our faith is strengthened, and we begin to hope for more, for a sound in the air, for a sign unmistakable and clear - for a patient daisy. God is a lover and leads us artfully, attracting us, then showering us with blessings, then withdrawing to start the process all over again on a new level."[1]

   [*pause*]

Unlike the movies, these sequels are just as exciting as the original. Why? Precisely because they answer that ages-old question - is God really here, does God really exist? In awe and fear, Jacob answers, "How awesome is this place! This is none other than the house of God!"

Yes, this is a sequel and the main character is clear; it's God - YHWH - "the God of Abraham your father and the God of Isaac." And there will be more sequels in this library we call the Bible - in fact, we've got one coming up soon - if I remember right, the title was 'Thin Spaces 8 - Moses and the Burning Bush' - it was a real blockbuster. In fact, I think there's a sequel in development right now, in our time and our place - a 'thin space' somewhere we will never know - until it happens - and we respond. But there's one thing we can always count on - that awesome main character remains the same - always and forever.

And that, indeed, is good news. Amen.

[1] Murray Bodo, *Song of the Sparrow*, St. Anthony Messenger Press, 1976, p. 6-7.

Be Prepared
Matthew 25:1-13

25 "Then the kingdom of heaven will be like this. Ten bridesmaids took their lamps and went to meet the bridegroom. 2 Five of them were foolish, and five were wise. 3 When the foolish took their lamps, they took no oil with them; 4 but the wise took flasks of oil with their lamps. 5 As the bridegroom was delayed, all of them became drowsy and slept. 6 But at midnight there was a shout, 'Look! Here is the bridegroom! Come out to meet him.' 7 Then all those bridesmaids got up and trimmed their lamps. 8 The foolish said to the wise, 'Give us some of your oil, for our lamps are going out.' 9 But the wise replied, 'No! there will not be enough for you and for us; you had better go to the dealers and buy some for yourselves.' 10 And while they went to buy it, the bridegroom came, and those who were ready went with him into the wedding banquet; and the door was shut. 11 Later the other bridesmaids came also, saying, 'Lord, lord, open to us.' 12 But he replied, 'Truly I tell you, I do not know you.' 13 Keep awake therefore, for you know neither the day nor the hour.

"Be prepared." When I was a boy scout, I heard this a lot. Be prepared with plant and animal knowledge to be safe when we were out in the woods. Be prepared for emergencies by learning first aid skills. Be prepared for hiking by having the right shoes and socks. Be prepared for long hikes with the right pack, sleeping bag, tent, etc., etc. Whatever it was, we were gonna be prepared for it!

Today, we formally offer our stewardship pledges and thank God for this creation we are a part of and of which we are called to be stewards. In a sense then, our pledges are part of how we prepare for the next year - it's our way of 'being prepared.' We've tried to cover all our bases - we've got staff expenses, utilities, insurance - paper and toner cartridges, stamps and birthday postcards, worship supplies. What else? Oh yes! Music! And cleaning. Then there's the evangelism committee and Christian education expenses - and everything else we can plan for.

Working out a budget and trying to stick to it is good planning, isn't it? Even as families we have to do that. You don't want to end up like the fellow who said, "Well, I reached the end of my money for this month - but I haven't reached the end of my month yet!"

[*pause*]

It's good to be prepared. That's what the author of Matthew wants his listeners to know; he says, "Keep awake, therefore, for you know neither the day nor the hour." The author wants us to frame this morality tale in terms of who's prepared and who isn't prepared. It's a story of 10 bridesmaids - must be a pretty big wedding to have that many bridesmaids - did they all have to buy their own dresses? Anyway, for some reason, they've all got lamps but half of them brought extra oil too. Now, the bridegroom is delayed so they all take a nap! This sounds awfully strange to me but hey, it's not my wedding!

Then finally, the bridegroom shows up - but it's midnight! [*pause*] Once again, it's not my wedding - I'm just sayin'! So they all wake up and 'trim their lamps'. Now apparently, they've all run their lamps down on fuel - while they were napping! - but five of them have extra oil so they just refill their lamps; the other five have to run off to the local lamp oil merchant to buy more oil - because the five who have oil won't share any with them - they're afraid there won't be enough for any of them then. Now wait a second - it's midnight - what lamp oil merchant's even going to be open at this hour? I'm almost completely sure they didn't have 24-hour Walmart's in Palestine back then!

As unbelievable as it seems, they find someone to sell them oil and hurry back, but when they get back to the wedding banquet, the bridegroom won't let them in - he claims to not know them now! What? He's forgotten them in an hour. This story's just - weird, isn't it?

I really don't like this story. Besides being downright confusing, it's got a dark side to it that I find bothersome and slightly offensive. First, where's the bride in all this? If she and this so-called 'bridegroom' set up the whole wedding with 10 bridesmaids, wouldn't they notice when there's only 5 who actually come in? Wouldn't the bride be just a tad mad at 5 of her best friends being kept out?

And why are the 5 who didn't bring extra oil called foolish? Should they have known this bridegroom would be late? Had he been married before and shown up late? Then when the bridegroom finally shows up, why didn't the ones with extra oil share some? The five without extra oil aren't broke - they could easily reimburse their friends - they have the money to go buy oil. And when they went into the wedding banquet, didn't the bridegroom have the place lit up? What would they need their own lamps for at a wedding banquet?

You know what? I just don't like this story very much. It's not really a parable, there's no reversal of social position - and it's mean-spirited. And it's not really about being prepared at all - it may just be me but it seems to be more about being lucky with a capricious and flakey bridegroom! I'm not alone in feeling this way, listen to what current scholarship has to say about this particular text:

"The parable of the ten maidens or the closed door, as it is variously known, may derive from common lore in the ancient Near East, or it may have been created by the evangelist. Scholars are confident of this assessment for two reasons: (1) this story does not comport with other parables of Jesus and his use of language generally; (2) the context in which this parable appears in Matthew is strongly apocalyptic.

This story does not have any of the earmarks of Jesus' authentic parables. It does not cut against the religious and social grain. Rather, it confirms common wisdom: those who are prepared will succeed, those not prepared will fail. Consequently, it does not surprise or shock; there is no unexpected twist in the story; it comes out as one suspects, given the opening statement that five of the maidens were wise and five foolish. The story lacks humor, exaggeration, and paradox: it is straightforward, unimaginative, and moralizing (preparedness is rewarded). Although it utilizes concrete visual images, its application is obvious. In sum, there is nothing distinctive about it.

In addition, the parable emphasizes the social boundaries between those "inside" and those "outside": the closed door makes a definitive boundary. Jesus was more interested in breaking down social barriers than he was in erecting them. This parable contradicts that major premise of Jesus' authentic parables and aphorisms. In contrast, the parable fits hand in glove with Matthew's own perspective, which is to separate the sheep from the goats (Matt 25:31-46), to distinguish those who deserve to be admitted to the wedding banquet from those who are not properly attired (Matt 22:1-14). The parable of the ten maidens thus seems to illustrate Matthew's understanding of the gospel rather than Jesus' vision of God's domain."[1]

What in the world can this text say to us today? You know, the ironic thing is I think the author nailed it with that final verse, "Keep awake therefore, for you know neither the day nor the hour." Well, that's just great - how can you prepare for something you know nothing about? How can you prepare for something - you can't prepare for?

[*pause*]

Our service and stewardship - our response to God's grace - everyday - is part of our preparation for the unknown. It's what we do in response to Jesus' love.

Notwithstanding Matthew's morality tale, we know God's giving a banquet - and God wants everyone to come! So let go of your fears, follow the recipe - Jesus is bringing the extra oil for us - we'll 'slide right in'!

And that - is good news! Amen.

---

[1] Funk, R. W., Hoover, R. W. and The Jesus Seminar, *The Five Gospels*, HarperSanFrancisco, 1993, p. 254.

A Letter from Home
Gal 6:7-16

7 Do not be deceived; God is not mocked, for you reap whatever you sow. 8 If you sow to your own flesh, you will reap corruption from the flesh; but if you sow to the Spirit, you will reap eternal life from the Spirit. 9 So let us not grow weary in doing what is right, for we will reap at harvest time if we do not give up. 10 So then, whenever we have an opportunity, let us work for the good of all, and especially for those of the family of faith.

11 See what large letters I make when I am writing in my own hand! 12 It is those who want to make a good showing in the flesh that try to compel you to be circumcised—only that they may not be persecuted for the cross of Christ. 13 Even the circumcised do not themselves obey the law, but they want you to be circumcised so that they may boast about your flesh. 14 May I never boast of anything except the cross of our Lord Jesus Christ, by which[a] the world has been crucified to me, and I to the world. 15 For neither circumcision nor uncircumcision is anything; but a new creation is everything! 16 As for those who will follow this rule—peace be upon them, and mercy, and upon the Israel of God.

[This unique sermon consists of two parts. First, a brief homily in outline form, designed to be enriched and fleshed out by the preacher as it is presented. The centerpiece is a 'letter' to the current church community written as though the Apostle Paul was writing to us today. This 'letter' can be printed on yellowed paper and rolled as a scroll to mimic authenticity. Here it is presented in a different font to accomplish the same effect]

1. This letter differs from Paul's other letters - most have warm, friendly intros and conclusions - not this one!

- Rather than an inspirational conclusion, Paul can't let it go - he reiterates the gist of the letter again!

- He's angry, afraid, worried, incensed... his friends might give up their freedom in Christ to be slaves to the law...

- We know something about freedom... particularly on the 4th of July!

2. <u>Declaration of Independence - July 4, 1776</u>

We hold these truths to be self-evident, that all men are created equal, that they are endowed by their Creator with certain unalienable Rights, that among these are Life, Liberty and the pursuit of Happiness.

3. <u>Bill of Rights - Dec. 15, 1791</u>

First Amendment: Congress shall make no law respecting an establishment of religion, or prohibiting the free exercise thereof; or abridging the freedom of speech, or of the press; or the right of the people peaceably to assemble, and to petition the Government for a redress of grievances.

4. Even our frontier church knows this - Barton Stone and several other Presbyterian ministers broke from their denomination precisely because they were forced to follow rules, obey the church's "laws" ...

<u>Last Will and Testament of The Springfield Presbytery - June 28, 1804</u>

Imprimis. We *will*, that this body die, be dissolved, and sink into union with the Body of Christ at large; for there is but one body, and one Spirit, even as we are called in one hope of our calling.

Item. We *will*, that our power of making laws for the government of the church, and executing them by delegated authority, forever cease; that the people may have free course to the Bible, and adopt *the law of the Spirit of life in Christ Jesus.*

5. What if Paul had written to us? What if the Christian Church (Disciples of Christ) in Nebraska started making rules for the individual churches?

What if - in 1892 after the first Disciples' minister came to Grand Island and started First Christian Church, somebody else came and said, "No, you're not doing it right, you've got to follow *these* rules if you want to *truly* be the church...

6. Amazingly, a letter has been found - maybe coincidence, maybe miracle - who knows? A letter from Paul to the churches in Nebraska!

To the churches in Nebraska:

Grace and peace to you from God our Creator and the Lord Jesus Christ, who gave himself for our sins to rescue us from the mess we're in! Amen.

What is going on with you? I'm blown away to hear that you're deserting the grace of Christ and are turning so fast to a different gospel - which is really no gospel at all! Evidently somebody's throwing you into confusion and trying to pervert the gospel of Christ. I said it before and I'll say it again: If anybody is preaching to you a gospel other than what you already received and accepted, you can tell them to go to Hell!

You need to know, friends, that the gospel I preached is not something that I or anybody else made up. I didn't get it from anybody; I didn't learn it in a school, I received it by revelation from Jesus Christ!

You know what I was like before, how I wanted to destroy the church of God. But when God, who set me apart from birth and called me by grace, was pleased to reveal Jesus in me so that I might preach him among the Nebraskans, I didn't consult anybody, I didn't go to Lincoln to see those who were apostles before me, instead, I went immediately into Kansas and later returned to Omaha.

It was three years after then that I went to Lincoln to get acquainted with Peter; I stayed with him fifteen days but I didn't see anybody else except James, the Lord's brother. This is no lie. No one in the churches of Nebraska that are in Christ knew me personally. Sure, they knew about me - and they praised God because of me: "The man who formerly persecuted us is now preaching the faith he once tried to destroy."

I used to think the most important thing was to follow the rules, to do things the right way, but that won't work. We're not washed clean and innocent by following laws but by faith in Jesus Christ. We've put our faith in Christ Jesus that we may be innocent by faith in Christ and not by following some set of rules, because no one looks innocent that way - it'd be like a banker claiming innocence because he 'followed the rules' that said it was okay to give out mortgages without proof of income!

But what if, while we're seeking to be innocent in Christ, it becomes obvious that we ourselves are sinners, does that mean that Christ promotes sin? No way! If I go back to trying to follow rules, that just makes me a rule-breaker. I died to the rules so that I might live for God. It's like I've been crucified with Christ so I no longer live, but rather it's Christ who lives in me. The life I live now, I live by faith in the Son of God, who loved me and gave himself for me. I don't set aside the grace of God, for if righteousness could be gained by following the rules, Christ died for nothing! And I don't believe Christ died for nothing!

You foolish Nebraskans! Who's pulled the wool over your eyes? Before those very eyes Jesus Christ was clearly portrayed as crucified. I want to learn just one thing from you: Did you receive the Spirit by following the rules, or by believing what you heard? Are you so foolish? After beginning with the Spirit, are you now trying to attain your goal by human effort? Have you suffered so much for nothing—if it really was for nothing? Does God give you the Spirit and work miracles among you because you follow the rules, or because you believe what you heard?

Before this faith came, we were held prisoners by the rules, locked up until faith should be revealed. Now that faith has come, we're no longer under the supervision of rules. You are all children of God through faith in Christ Jesus, for all of you who were baptized into Christ have clothed yourselves with Christ. There is neither Kansan nor Nebraskan, slave nor free, male nor female, for you are all one in Christ Jesus.

Why? It's for freedom that Christ has set us free! Stand your ground, then, and don't let yourselves be roped again to a slavery to rules. You, my brothers and sisters, were called to be free. But don't use your freedom to do whatever you want; rather, serve one another in love. All the rules can be summed up in a single command: "Love your neighbor as yourself." If you keep on biting and picking on each other, watch out or you'll be destroyed by each other - what goes around, comes around...

So I say, live by the Spirit, and you won't have to gratify the desires of the sinful nature. For the sinful nature desires what's contrary to the Spirit, and the Spirit wants what's contrary to the sinful nature. They're in conflict with each other, so that you don't do what you want. But if you're led by the Spirit, you're not under the rules.

The sinful stuff is obvious: sexual immorality, impurity and debauchery; idolatry; hatred, discord, jealousy, fits of rage, selfish ambition, dissensions, factions and envy; drunkenness, orgies, and the like. I'm telling you, just like I did before, if you live like this, you will not inherit the kingdom of God.

But the fruit of the Spirit is love, joy, peace, patience, kindness, goodness, faithfulness, gentleness and self-control. You know there's no rules against these. Those who belong to Christ Jesus have crucified the sinful nature with its passions and desires. Since we live by the Spirit, let's keep in step with the Spirit.

Don't try to fool yourselves: God cannot be mocked. A person reaps what they sow. The one who sows to please his sinful nature will reap destruction; the one who sows to please the Spirit, will reap eternal life. Let's not become weary of doing good, for when the time comes, we'll reap a mighty harvest, if we don't give up. So whenever we can, let's do good to all people, especially to those who belong to the family of believers.

So finally, I've just got to say it once again, it's those who want to make a good impression outwardly that are trying to make you follow rules. And the only reason they do this is to avoid being persecuted for the cross of Christ. Not even those who subscribe to the rules obey the rules, yet they want you to so that they may boast about you! May I never boast except in the cross of our Lord Jesus Christ, through which the world has been crucified to me, and I to the world. Christ didn't die for nothing; for freedom, Christ has set us free!

May the grace of our Lord Jesus Christ be with your spirit, brothers and sisters. Amen.

7. What a heritage we have! Let us not forget our heritage, not on this 4th of July when we celebrate the birth of our nation. A nation founded on the belief that their Creator endowed them with 'certain unalienable rights', and that this nation may make 'no law respecting an establishment of religion, or prohibiting the free exercise thereof', and that our very tradition was founded on the principle that 'our power of making laws for the government of the church, and

executing them by delegated authority, forever cease; that the people may have free course to the Bible, and adopt *the law of the Spirit of life in Christ Jesus.*'

- For freedom, Christ has set us free! Let us pray our nation continues to remember this - so that Paul no longer needs to send letters like this!

Amen!

The Illusion of Salvation
Luke 23:33-43

33 When they came to the place that is called The Skull, they crucified Jesus there with the criminals, one on his right and one on his left. [[34 Then Jesus said, "Father, forgive them; for they do not know what they are doing."]] And they cast lots to divide his clothing. 35 And the people stood by, watching; but the leaders scoffed at him, saying, "He saved others; let him save himself if he is the Messiah of God, his chosen one!" 36 The soldiers also mocked him, coming up and offering him sour wine, 37 and saying, "If you are the King of the Jews, save yourself!" 38 There was also an inscription over him, "This is the King of the Jews."

39 One of the criminals who were hanged there kept deriding him and saying, "Are you not the Messiah? Save yourself and us!" 40 But the other rebuked him, saying, "Do you not fear God, since you are under the same sentence of condemnation? 41 And we indeed have been condemned justly, for we are getting what we deserve for our deeds, but this man has done nothing wrong." 42 Then he said, "Jesus, remember me when you come into your kingdom." 43 He replied, "Truly I tell you, today you will be with me in Paradise."

What does 'saved' mean when you're hanging on a cross? That's the first thing that popped into my head as I sat with this text this week. That - and my friend, Tommy.

You remember my friend, Tommy, don't you? Tommy, who lived out servanthood so well - just doin' what he ought to do? For those of you who might've missed that sermon, I met Tommy when I lived for a short time in Spencerville, a quiet little town that's on the way to wherever you're going. Everybody knew Tommy - Red down at Red's Tire and Auto Service, Elvira down at the Buttermilk Cafe` - everybody knew Tommy. But nobody really knew him either. You see, Tommy never played it safe.

He didn't hang around long. He was here, there - and - then he was gone! But he kinda rubbed off on you and you couldn't help but respond. [*chuckle*] He'd always straighten and bus the table when we met at the Cafe` and I still stack my dishes up whenever I'm out to eat. I still dump my pocket change in the Salvation Army bucket - just seems like I ought to do it. I want to tell another odd thing about Tommy. Like I said, he never played it safe.

I'm not sure but I'm guessing Bartlesville is a lot like Spencerville. There's lots of churches here, just like there were there. There was the big Baptist church right in the center of town with the big Presbyterian church just around the corner. Most of the other brand name Protestant churches were represented too. And there, growing like a corn field on a sunny July day, was the nondenominational church that'd taken over an old Target store out in the mall on the edge of town. Oh, they wouldn't be there long - they already had some property to the south and a big sign saying, "Future Home of ..." well, I don't quite recall their name - but it was gonna be their new home someday!

On the other side of the railroad tracks which ran through the center of Spencerville, there was a little church in the old Feed store that served the Latino community. I heard Tommy used to go there sometimes. Ohh, Tommy' d gone to all the big churches and smiled and brought something to each potluck dinner he'd attended. He fit in well no matter whether under the beautiful stained-glass windows at the Baptist church or the solemn ritual and liturgy at the Episcopal church. Just between you and me, Tommy once told me how they all thought they had something special but he didn't see much difference between them! They each thought their potlucks were the best but he liked them all!

And I suppose it would've been easy for Tommy to just keep going to one of those bigger churches - but he didn't. I asked Tommy why he went to the little church and you know what he said? He said, "Folks who get evicted and need a place to stay mostly don't go to the big churches." I heard a rumor once that one of those needy folks Tommy' d given a cot to had robbed him - stolen his TV and pawned it. Tommy kept going to the little church anyway - that was one of the things he did that made people think he was odd even as they liked him. Tommy didn't play it safe - and that was sometimes scary to be around.

[pause]

But you know, throughout the history of Judaism and Christianity, there's been lots and lots of folks who didn't play it safe. Take David - he took on Goliath with some rocks and a sling - I sure wouldn't call that 'safe', yet he was loved by God, in spite of his all too human failings. Then there's John the Baptist. Not only did he preach, he did it in the wilderness with nothing but grasshoppers and honey to eat. Now that sounds downright repulsive, let alone unsafe!

It doesn't get better as we come forward either. James and Peter and Stephen and Paul were all martyred - they didn't play it safe. And the surprising thing is these martyrs faced their martyrdom with courage and in some cases, even joy! And this just flat baffled the Roman authorities. Why wouldn't it? These crazy Christians looked like atheists to the Romans - they refused to show allegiance to the Emperor/God and instead chose to follow an invisible 'God', of all things. Who ever heard of such nonsense?

In the year 107, the bishop of Antioch, Ignatius, was condemned to death by the imperial authorities. Now, by this time, he was nearly 80 years old; all he had to do was swear allegiance to the Emperor and he'd be set free. But he wrote to the Christians in Rome who were suggesting they could free him, saying, "If you remain silent about me, I shall become a word of God. But if you allow yourselves to be swayed by the love in which you hold my flesh, I shall again be no more than a human voice."

[*shake my head*]

All he had to do was swear to the Emperor and he'd been safe.

One of the people Ignatius wrote to was Polycarp, the bishop of Smyrna. In the year 155, he suffered the same fate as Ignatius. Again the judge insisted, promising that if he would swear by the Emperor and curse Christ, he would be free to go. But Polycarp replied, "For eighty-six years I have served him, and he has done me no evil. How could I curse my king, who *saved* me?"

Neither Ignatius nor Polycarp played it safe.

[*pause*]

You know another character who didn't play it safe? Francis of Assisi. And he had it safe and easy! He was the son of a prosperous fabric merchant and no one loved the good life like young Francis. He could party with the best of them; he was the prime favorite of the young nobles of Assisi, the best at any kind of arms; the very king of frolic! But he was captured during one of the skirmishes with a rival city and was held for a year. During that time, he became ill and began to question the emptiness of his life. Eventually, he declared he was going to take a wife of surpassing fairness - Lady Poverty. The story is told that as he was crossing the Umbrian plain on horseback, he came upon a poor leper. The sudden appearance of this repulsive person filled him with disgust and he instinctively retreated, but, overcoming his fear, he dismounted, embraced the leper and gave him all the money he had. After mounting his horse, he looked back - and the leper was gone! Francis understood his encounter as an encounter with the living God, with Christ. Francis decided to follow Christ's example and give all he had away. He actually went to his father's warehouses and took a load of expensive fabric, sold it, and gave all the money to the church at the foot of the town!

Dad was so incensed, he dragged Francis home, beat and bound him and locked him in a closet! Eventually, he even wanted to disown him. This Francis was happy to do, so there, right in front of the bishop, he stripped all of his clothes off and gave them back to his father saying, "Hitherto I have called you my father on earth; henceforth I desire to say only 'Our Father who art in heaven.'

Of course, we know him today as St. Francis. He had it safe - but he didn't play it safe! Do you know what Francis thought not playing it safe was? Courtesy! I think Tommy would appreciate this. To Francis, courtesy was part of justice; he found it to be one of the qualities of God who, "of his courtesy, gives His sun and His rain to the just and the unjust." This habit of courtesy Francis taught his disciples. "Whoever may come to us," he wrote, "whether a friend or a foe, a thief or a robber, let him be kindly received." The feasts he spread for the starving brigands in the forest of Monte Casals were ample proof that "as he taught, so he wrought."

You see, doing the "safe" thing isn't the same as "being saved." And "being saved" doesn't mean we'll be "safe." That's the illusion of salvation, that it's a safe thing. Salvation is a freely given gift of God - it's not something we earn but rather something we respond to! And it certainly isn't safe! The whole ritual of baptism is a ritualistic death and rebirth in Christ in recognition of God's grace. To paraphrase Barbara Brown Taylor: salvation is a transformed way of life in the world, that is characterized by peace, meaning and freedom. Salvation happens as a result of our repentance - a turning away from our old way of life and turning toward a new way that promises more abundant life. That's what St. Francis did when he turned to poverty, what the early martyrs did when they turned to Christ; that's what Tommy did somewhere in his earlier life before I knew him. And that's why they had a freedom to *not* play it safe.

Now don't get me wrong, there's nothing wrong with *being* safe, with being concerned with the safety of loved ones, with going to the doctor and taking our medicines - of course those are valid concerns. But "salvation" is a freedom that goes beyond life - beyond death - if you're "saved", "safe" doesn't mean the same thing anymore, does it? And boy, Jesus gave us plenty of examples in his parables to try to get this across. From the very beginning of Jesus' ministry where he says to Peter and Andrew, "Follow me, and I will make you fish for people," they do the totally unsafe thing - they follow him! In fact, the very first word Matthew puts on Jesus' lips as he starts his ministry in Matthew 4:17, is: "Repent, for the kingdom of heaven has come near." He never says, "Play it safe!"

And how about the rich young man who wants to join Jesus? Jesus welcomes him and offers him salvation. All he has to do is turn from his old life - do the totally unsafe thing and give up his riches - and he can't do it. He's more concerned with "being safe" than "being saved." Then there's the parable of the wealthy farmer who builds extra barns so he can play it safe and store up grain for his future - only to die that night! Of course, you can't forget about the ruler who gives money into the care of three servants then goes off on a long trip. When he returns, it's the one who played it safe that ends up losing! That's why Peter cries bitterly when he hears the cock crow three times - he knows he's played it safe.

Doing the safe thing isn't the same as being saved.

To Jesus, being saved is the vastly more important thing. Remember the story about the paralytic man? How they wanted to bring him to Jesus for healing but the crowds were so thick, they had to rip a hole in the roof and lower him down on ropes? Right off the bat, that doesn't sound too safe to me! But what does Jesus do? Does he heal him right away? No! The first thing he does is forgive his sins - he "saves" him! And the woman who risks being beaten by the crowd so she can touch the hem of his robe? She's already saved; her faith has made her well. Over and over, Jesus does the risky thing, the unsafe thing, and offers salvation. No, Jesus never played it safe - because he was saved already! His ministry was a repetition of this very theme; he's told us over and over - way before we ever get to the place called 'The Skull', Jesus has told us doing the safe thing isn't the same as being saved.

What does 'saved' look like when you're hanging on a cross? What does 'saved' mean when you're hanging on a cross? It means not having to answer fool questions about safety, that's what it means! It looks like martyrs facing death courageously, even joyfully. It looks like a nurse helping an AIDS victim, it looks like St. Francis eating off the same platter with lepers, it looks like volunteers at Salvation Army feeding Thanksgiving dinner to the homeless, it looks like warm clothes and gifts out of a shoebox for a needy child at Christmas, it looks like food taken to CONCERN - it looks like everything we do that flies in the face of what society might consider good sense! It looks like - not playing it safe!

Jesus doesn't respond to the taunts - they miss the point anyway. He doesn't have to "save himself" - he's already saved! And because he's saved, he's free to not worry about his safety. Why do you think he doesn't offer salvation to the criminal who asks to be remembered - because the criminal's repented - he's already saved - *that's* why he'll be with Jesus in paradise that very day!

No, Jesus didn't need to respond to the leaders and the soldiers and the scornful criminal when they said, "Save yourself!" But I think if he had, he might've said, "What do you want? Do you want to be saved? Or do you just want to play it safe?"

Amen.

The Sound of Giving
Matthew 6:1-4

"Beware of practicing your piety before others in order to be seen by them; for then you have no reward from your Father in heaven. 2 "So whenever you give alms, do not sound a trumpet before you, as the hypocrites do in the synagogues and in the streets, so that they may be praised by others. Truly I tell you, they have received their reward. 3 But when you give alms, do not let your left hand know what your right hand is doing, 4 so that your alms may be done in secret; and your Father who sees in secret will reward you.

It's so hard to figure out what to say about stewardship. It's so hard to talk about giving - seems like there's someone every other week with a plea for support. How do we figure out what to do? Well, as it turns out, the people back in ancient times had the same sort of problem. I guess we've always had the problem of uneven distribution of resources.

The Israelites were admonished repeatedly to take care of the poor; the whole concept of the sabbatical year and jubilee are derived from the idea that whatever we have is ultimately from God and God wants it to be shared by everyone. Actually, this concept can be traced all the way back to the creation story. No - not that first one we all like to hang on to about us having dominion - rather that second creation story, the one about stewardship. Take a look at Gen. 2:15, "The Lord God took the man and put him in the garden of Eden to till it and keep it." We're supposed to be the stewards of the land; it's not just for us. This gets reflected in Exodus 23:10-11, "For six years you shall sow your land and gather in its yield; but the seventh year you shall let it rest and lie fallow, so that the poor of your people may eat; and what they leave the wild animals may eat. You shall do the same with your vineyard, and with your olive orchard." We're supposed to be stewards not solely to take care of ourselves, but to take care of the poor as well.

And again in Leviticus 19:9-10, "When you reap the harvest of your land, you shall not reap to the very edges of your field or gather the gleanings of your harvest. You shall not strip your vineyard bare or gather the fallen grapes of your vineyard; you shall leave them for the poor and the alien: I am the Lord your God."

You see? These are simply commandments that come out of our responsibility for taking care of God's creation. And this gets expressed in even more modern terms in Deuteronomy 15:7-11 that we can certainly understand: "If there is among you anyone in need, a member of your community in any of your towns within the land that the Lord your God is giving you, do not be hard-hearted or tight-fisted toward your needy neighbor. You should rather open your hand, willingly lending enough to meet the need, whatever it may be. Be careful that you do not entertain a mean thought, thinking, 'The seventh year, the year of remission is near,' and therefore view your needy neighbor with hostility and give nothing; your neighbor might cry to the Lord against you, and you would incur guilt. Give liberally and be ungrudging when you do so, for on this account the Lord your God will bless you in all your work and in all that you undertake. Since there will never cease to be some in need on the earth, I therefore command you, "Open your hand to the poor and needy neighbor in your land."

Boy, there's not a lot of wiggle room in that one, is there?! "Since there will never cease to be some in need on the earth, I therefore command you, "Open your hand to the poor and needy neighbor in your land."

Open your hand.

[pause]

So now Jesus is preaching, probably a thousand years later, and again it's about giving. What about 'open your hand' didn't they get? What has gone on so that even Jesus might echo the admonition, "You just don't get it!"

Well, let's do a little exegetical work first. Our text for today comes from the Sermon on the Mount. We went through it carefully over the whole summer so we know this sermon functions as a call to discipleship. In Matthew's gospel, it's Jesus' first big teaching sermon - he's got his disciples gathered around him - he's giving them instructions in detail: "So whenever you give alms, don't toot your own horn like the hypocrites do..."

This is just one of several repeating lessons that all make the comparison to hypocrites, saying, 'don't do like the hypocrites'. Don't give alms like the hypocrites, don't pray like the hypocrites, don't fast like the hypocrites. The greek word that's translated as hypocrites is always the same - 'hypocrites'. Strong's Concordance gives the definition as "an actor under an assumed character, a stage-player, i.e., a dissembler." Today, we might disparagingly say a politician or a TV evangelist. It's stereotypical - we know what it means. It's that pandering to your audience. It's like the Pharisee a few weeks ago who was more interested in those around him and how he looked than in praying quietly to God.

It's like that friend we all have who tells us they'll call - because they think that's what we want to hear - but they never do call, do they? It's like when

I say yes to someone's request because I know they want me to - but then I don't follow through. It's like when we pledge to do something but don't actually do it. It's like offering something - then closing the hand tightly to hold on to it. [*pause*] Yeah, it's like that.

It'd even be like, well, like the scripture today, sounding the trumpet before me as I bring my offering to the collection plate....

[*trumpet plays loudly; I take out cash and parade it to offering plate*]

Now that's just silly, isn't it? We'd never be so foolish as to give our offerings like that would we? Well, neither would the religious leaders back in ancient times. That's the difficult thing - this wasn't meant to be a real example, any more so than the next one, "don't let your left hand know what your right hand is doing..." They're both paradoxes - how can you not know what your hands are doing - left or right? How do you keep that in secret?

I don't know. I'm serious folks - I don't know how you do that. I'm hoping some of you do - 'cause that's your challenge for this week. I want you to think about it and let me know what you think it means - this paradox of not letting your left hand know what the right is doing.

Ohh, I've got a few ideas about it - I think it could have something to do with God's earlier command, "Open your hands." I don't know but I think that 'open your hands' might look something like this:

- Giving change to the Salvation Army at Christmas
- Fixing sack lunches and buying supplies for CONCERN
- Buying equipment/supplies and simply donating it to the church
- Paying my pledge in cash when no one's looking
- Giving money to Church World Service in addition to whatever else I'm doing.
- Special offerings
- Buying Event tickets then giving them away

It's about giving on the spur of the moment, it's about not budgeting giving - it's about opening my hand whenever the need arises. And it doesn't have to be money - it can be:

- Coming over early on a Sunday to shovel snow off the walks

- Picking up litter off the parking lot just 'cause it's there
- Sending someone a thank you card
- Cleaning a couple miles of roadway on a Saturday morning
- Calling someone just to say hi
- Taking our leftover Halloween candy to the Lighthouse Mission
- Smiling at a stranger and shaking their hand

[*pause*]

"Open your hand," God said. Open your hand. Don't look - don't check your bank balance, don't see who's watching... open your hand. And don't worry if it's your left or right hand. You know what I think? I think it means letting your heart be connected to your hand rather than your head. Let your love be connected to your hand rather than your logic. Let your love of God be connected to your hand.

[*pause*]

Paradoxes of which hand notwithstanding, doing what's easy is never enough; never has been. We've been called from the *beginning of creation* to be stewards - for everyone - on God's behalf. God said, "Open your hand." Don't even look which one it is.

May it be so always. Amen.

Little Is - As Little Does
Luke 19:1-10

19 He entered Jericho and was passing through it. 2 A man was there named Zacchaeus; he was a chief tax collector and was rich. 3 He was trying to see who Jesus was, but on account of the crowd he could not, because he was short in stature. 4 So he ran ahead and climbed a sycamore tree to see him, because he was going to pass that way. 5 When Jesus came to the place, he looked up and said to him, "Zacchaeus, hurry and come down; for I must stay at your house today." 6 So he hurried down and was happy to welcome him. 7 All who saw it began to grumble and said, "He has gone to be the guest of one who is a sinner." 8 Zacchaeus stood there and said to the Lord, "Look, half of my possessions, Lord, I will give to the poor; and if I have defrauded anyone of anything, I will pay back four times as much." 9 Then Jesus said to him, "Today salvation has come to this house, because he too is a son of Abraham. 10 For the Son of Man came to seek out and to save the lost."

I hear this text and it makes me think of a scene I recall from the movie, "Forrest Gump". In the scene, young Forrest has been teased in school and called stupid. But his mom tells him, "Stupid is as stupid does." The phrase suggests that *saying* someone's stupid doesn't *make* them stupid, their *actions* show whether they're stupid. I'm sure you've heard this sort of comparison. We might even apply it to ourselves: 'Christian is as Christian does'. Jesus would be all over that one, wouldn't he? The sermon on the mount is full of this, his parables are all over it and the tale of the sheep and goats in Matthew 25 - "Just as you did it to one of the least of these…, you did it to me," sums it up nicely… "Love your neighbor as yourself" maybe even better.

So I'm struck by this text today about a little man with a big stature, little Zacchaeus. He's a dreaded tax collector, and he's a 'chief' tax collector to boot! And he's short! So if he's true to stereotype, he's probably arrogant, whiney, boastful, a bully, and possibly obnoxious but what can you do? He's rich! But no matter how you slice it, when we first meet him, he's 'little' in every way possible! You know he's just trying to see Jesus so he can belittle him, decide he's just another one of those foolish itinerant preachers that wandered all over Galilee in those days. Zacchaeus has probably heard someone talking about Jesus and he wants some ammunition to put him down in the future. He's just there to dig up some dirt on Jesus. Yeah, he's arrogant alright, running and climbing a tree rather than being dignified and respectful but hey - he's rich - he doesn't care what people think of him! A thoroughly despicable character is little Zacchaeus.

[pause]

Here's another thing that intrigues me in this story. Initially, Jesus was "making his way through" the city. It doesn't sound like he has any intention of stopping. So why does Jesus notice Zacchaeus up there in the tree? Why does he say, "I must be your guest today?" Who knows? Maybe something made him change his mind, change his plans - maybe the disciples needed a break. Or maybe he looked up and saw Zacchaeus and something about Zacchaeus said to Jesus, "help me".

So then the most interesting thing in the whole story happens. Jesus looks up into Zacchaeus' eyes and says, "Zacchaeus, hurry and come down; for I must stay at your house today." Jesus is saying, "help me." to Zacchaeus. And, against all stereotypes, Zacchaeus hops down out of his sycamore tree - happy to serve Jesus! And not only that, he's going to give his riches away and make restitution that's beyond what the local customs would've required! This arrogant, little man has been transformed! Now - change isn't easy. We all know this - 'you can take the boy out of the country but, you can't take the country out of the boy' is a typical way of saying it. So how do we know Zacchaeus has changed? His *actions* have changed.

Little is - as little does.

[*pause*]

Another story: a girl, a young woman really - beautiful, long silky hair and a teenager's smooth skin, intelligent and friendly - she had her whole life in front of her - she got blinded by love, or, maybe it was passion? Anyway, a young man, just a boy really, swept her away. Her plans for college and a career got pushed aside, for they were in love - so much so that they decided they didn't even need to get married. Love would be enough.

[*sigh*]

You know what happened next. She found herself pregnant. At first, it was exciting! She was going to have a little baby! Of course, her family wasn't very happy but everyone put on a brave face and gritted their respective teeth. Ohh, there were problems. The young man, a boy really, didn't handle it well and became verbally abusive with a threat of violence too. "You care more for that baby than you do for me!" "I don't care that you're tired - bring me another beer!" "Where've I been? Out with my buddies - what business is it of yours? I'll do whatever I want!"

Oh, she cried herself to sleep too many nights. "But - I love him." "He's really not so bad - he's sweet sometimes and he's trying." "Don't worry - he'll change when the baby comes."

Well - in due time, the baby did come. And she was a beautiful, wonderful baby girl! With perfect little feet and toes and perfect little fingers and fingernails and a soft down on her crown that hinted at the lovely auburn hair she'd grow into. And when that young woman, a mother now, looked down into her daughter's eyes - eyes that opened and looked straight at her as if to say, "Help me, hold me," her heart melted - and she was changed; she was transformed.

Oh, she went home at first thinking all the same hopes - that the father would change - grow up. But the tirades continued and the nights out continued - and she knew. She acted and left then - left him to find his own transformation. She's going to take care of her baby and give her everything she can - give that little baby her time and her money - whatever it takes.

Little is - as little does.

    [*pause*]

Another mother - in a different town and a different time - thinks and worries to herself. "Where is he? His car is here in front of the apartment - but there's no answer at the door. What if? What if - he's hurt? Oh, I hope he's not using drugs." "Why won't he answer?"

She's driven by this apartment so many times - and not found her son - so many times, that she's taken to driving different routes so she won't have to face her fears. The cellphone rings and she think, "Pick up - please pick up..." But there's no answer. She can't forget the day she first looked into *his* eyes - such a sweet, little baby boy with shining eyes that said, "Help me." She was changed that day - but now - that little baby, a young man now, needs help - he needs change.

So she tries one more time, walking slowly up the dingy steps, praying 'God, help me - help me find my son', she rings the old doorbell - "ring! ring!" and waits... and the door cracks open. Her son looks shaken and beat up but through the shakes and tears, he tells her he'd been angry at God, blaming God for the pain in his life. He'd hollered, "God if you're really here, do something! Send someone or something! I can't take it anymore!" And he said just then, the doorbell had rung.

Both their prayers were answered - and both were changed - deeply changed. He's back at work now. Oh, he should be a major league catcher the way he's had to handle all the curve balls life's thrown at him! Things' still tough but he's changed now; his actions have changed. He's not the same person he was on that lonely night.

Little is - as little does - even with little, one day at a time, steps.

[*pause*]

I heard a story recently on the internet, I'm not even sure who sent this to me, but I was intrigued enough by it that I saved it:

A few years ago a group of salesmen went to a regional sales convention in Chicago. They had assured their wives that they would be home in plenty of time for Friday night's dinner. In their rush, with tickets and briefcases, one of these salesmen inadvertently kicked over a table which held a display of apples. Apples flew everywhere. Without stopping or looking back, they all ran to reach the plane in time for their nearly missed boarding.

All but one! He paused, took a deep breath, got in touch with his feelings, and experienced a twinge of compassion for the girl whose apple stand had been overturned. "Go ahead'" he said as he waved. "Give Peggy a call and let her know I'll be late - I'll take the next available flight." Then he returned to the terminal where the apples were all over the terminal floor. He was glad he did.

The 16-year-old girl selling the apples was totally blind! She was softly crying, tears running down her cheeks in frustration, and at the same time helplessly groping for her spilled apples as the crowd swirled about her, no one stopping and no one seeming to care for her plight. But the salesman knelt on the floor with her, gathered up the apples, put them back on the table and helped organize her display. As he did this, he noticed that many of the apples were battered and bruised; these he set aside in another basket. When he had finished, he pulled out his wallet and said to the girl, "Here, please take this $40 for the damage we did. Are you okay?" She nodded through her tears. "I hope we didn't spoil your day too badly," he said. As he started to walk away, the bewildered blind girl called out to him, "Mister...." and then more softly, "Mister...are you Jesus?" He stopped in mid-stride, and he wondered. Then slowly he made his way to catch the later flight with that question burning and bouncing about in his soul: "Are you Jesus?" He was changed, transformed forever by the simple action of picking up apples.

Little is - as little does.

All were changed by their interaction with Jesus - *but not by his power.* You see, Jesus isn't doing miracles here and fixing everyone's problems, no, Jesus is the one crying out, "Hey! I need some help here!" He said to Zacchaeus, "I need to stay at your house today." He looked up through the eyes of a little baby girl as if to say, "Hold me; help me" and her mother was changed. He cried out from a young man's tortured soul to reassure a loving mother that her help was valuable. And he looked at the salesman through the eyes of a blind girl who said, "Are you Jesus?" With a powerful feeling of emotion and joy, they all were changed - forever. The salesman never forgot that question; the mothers loved and cared for their children all of their lives. Even little Zacchaeus, arrogant and skeptical but curious, was transformed. Whenever we're faced with an opportunity, with someone needing help, with someone too small to take care of themselves, we'll be faced with living up to the question - 'Are you Jesus?' We'll have to decide what actions we'll take.

Just remember - little is - as little does!

May it be so always. Amen.

Oceans of Hope
Luke 21:5-19

5 When some were speaking about the temple, how it was adorned with beautiful stones and gifts dedicated to God, he said, 6 "As for these things that you see, the days will come when not one stone will be left upon another; all will be thrown down."

7 They asked him, "Teacher, when will this be, and what will be the sign that this is about to take place?" 8 And he said, "Beware that you are not led astray; for many will come in my name and say, 'I am he!' and, 'The time is near!' Do not go after them.

9 "When you hear of wars and insurrections, do not be terrified; for these things must take place first, but the end will not follow immediately." 10 Then he said to them, "Nation will rise against nation, and kingdom against kingdom; 11 there will be great earthquakes, and in various places famines and plagues; and there will be dreadful portents and great signs from heaven.

12 "But before all this occurs, they will arrest you and persecute you; they will hand you over to synagogues and prisons, and you will be brought before kings and governors because of my name. 13 This will give you an opportunity to testify. 14 So make up your minds not to prepare your defense in advance; 15 for I will give you words and a wisdom that none of your opponents will be able to withstand or contradict. 16 You will be betrayed even by parents and brothers, by relatives and friends; and they will put some of you to death. 17 You will be hated by all because of my name. 18 But not a hair of your head will perish. 19 By your endurance you will gain your souls.

Well. That's a heck of a way to head towards Thanksgiving! This text is called, 'The Eschatological Discourse' - I'm guessing many of us don't use the word, eschatology, very often! Eschatology comes from two Greek words meaning "last" (ἔσχατος) and "study" (-λογία). It's the study of 'end things', whether the end of an individual life, the end of the age, the end of the world or the nature of the Kingdom of God. I think we're gonna need some context to try to understand this eschatological reading from Luke. First, let's look at a chronology of events relevant to the scripture.

<u>Slide</u>

Nero, persecution - 64 CE

Temple Destruction - 66-70 CE

Gospel of Mark - written ~70 CE

Vesuvius eruption - 79 CE

Gospel of Luke - written ~80 CE

Gospel of Matthew - written ~90CE

It's important to understand when the gospel accounts were written in order to understand what Luke wanted to say *in his time*. It's clear that Mark, along with the Q document, were primary sources for Luke and Matthew. Essentially, the author of Luke took the discourse from Mark and adapted it. Here's a concise description from *The People's New Testament Commentary* by Boring and Craddock: (264)

"We will deal with the distinctive lukan elements in Luke's adaptation of the Markan discourse for his own times, which may be summarized as follows: (1) The end of history will come. History is in God's hands and will not go on forever. God the Creator will bring history to a worthy conclusion. (2) The first Christian generation's understanding that they were living in the last times turned out to be mistaken. Terrible catastrophes and tragedies occurred in those days, including the persecution of Roman Christians by Nero in 64 CE, in which Christians were crucified and burned alive; the Jewish war against the Romans in 66-70 CE, which resulted in the destruction of Jerusalem and the temple, and the slaughter and enslavement of the city's population; the eruption of Vesuvius in 79 CE, which darkened the sky and changed the Mediterranean climate for a year. Many in the first Christian generation saw these events as signs of the end, but Luke looks back on them and can see that, terrible as they were, they were historical events, not signs of the end. (This is analogous to the way in which many Christians at the time of World War II saw the rise of Hitler, the Holocaust, the terrible events of the war, and the use of atomic weapons as signs that the second coming of Christ was near, but we may now look back on them as terrible events *in* history, not the end of history itself.). (3) The delay of the end and the reinterpretation of God's purpose in history is no reason for Christians to become complacent. The Jesus of Luke 21 calls for courageous testimony during the time of Christian mission, not speculation about when the end will come or indifference because its date cannot be predicted."[1]

So what do we do? Luke's text doesn't say when or what the end will actually be…but…, there is one place in the gospels where the last judgement is discussed - Matthew 25:31-46.

You know this text - it's the sheep and the goats! Jesus tells the sheep that they get to be part of the flock because they helped him when he was sick, and when he was naked and when he was jailed. The people said, "When did we do all that?" And Jesus says… (see if congregation will say it…) "As you did it to the least of these, you did it to me." Boring and Craddock note:

"Like the New Testament writers in general, despite his apocalyptic orientation Matthew has been very restrained in picturing what actually transpires when the Son of Man comes. This is the only scene in the New Testament with any details picturing the Last Judgement. To the reader's surprise (ancient and modern), the criterion of judgement is not confession of faith in Christ. Nothing is said of grace, justification, or the forgiveness of sins. What counts is whether or not one has acted with loving care for needy people. Such deeds are not a matter of "extra credit" but constitute the decisive criterion of judgement presupposed in all of chaps. 23-25, the weightier matters of the Law" of 23:23."[2]

Could 'loving care for needy people' be possible in terrible times? And might not that be the 'testimony' and the 'patience' that Luke points to in vs. 13 & 19? Might that tell us *what* to do even if we don't know *when* the end is?

[*pause*]

I grew up in the 50s. I can remember doing the drills where, in the event of a nuclear attack, we were to crawl under our desks and cover our heads with our hands. By the time I got to high school, of course, we'd rather cynically decided they might as well have told us to bend over and kiss a part of our anatomy goodbye! But we were *trying* to be prepared.

It was a time of fears about the threat of communism. What if the commies infiltrated us? What if they came in as immigrants? Senator Joseph McCarthy raised the proverbial red flag about infiltration of subversives into government posts and his methods fed a frenzy of 'red scare' fears and paranoia. Sadly, those 'methods' also ran roughshod over many people and, in the end, his tactics actually hindered efforts to safeguard security. But what if? Remember the Cuban missile crisis in October 1962?

Yeah, I remember that and the drills and I even remember fallout shelters. We didn't put one in - but a neighbor did. They dug a huge hole in the backyard - all of us neighborhood kids hoped they were putting in a swimming pool - but no, a big crane came and dropped a big piece of pipe into the ground then they covered it up with dirt. All that showed was a couple of ventilation pipes. I actually got to go into it once. It had a couple of bunk beds and a small desk and shelf unit. There was a pantry filled with canned goods and cereals. I have no idea if it would've done any good if there'd ever been a nuclear attack. Yet, in spite of all the hysteria, we neighbors were close to one another, *there was hope* in the midst of the turmoil and fear, and we were thankful for our neighbors.

By the way, right before I went off to college, they dug that shelter up and put in the swimming pool.

[*pause*]

Another example: In 1999, I had a computer, just like I do today. It met all of my needs and never gave me any problems. It didn't ask me to store water just in case it got sick, it didn't tell me to buy up batteries for my flashlights, candles for my mantle, or kerosene for my heater. But, apparently, lots of other people's computers were quite scared that they were going to suffer a nervous breakdown that New Year's Eve; people weren't taking any chances!

Do you remember this? It was known as the 'Y2K' bug[3] and experts speculated that computer programs could stop working or produce bad results because they stored years with only two digits and that the year 2000 would be represented by 00 and would be interpreted by software as the year 1900. This would cause date comparisons to produce incorrect results. Many also thought that embedded systems, making use of similar date logic, might fail and cause utilities and other crucial infrastructure to fail. And the media hype turned it into a doomsday scenario.

Special committees were set up by governments to monitor remedial work and contingency planning, particularly by crucial infrastructures such as telecommunications, utilities and the like, to ensure that the most critical services had fixed their own problems and were prepared for problems with others. Yet it was only the safe passing of the main "event horizon" itself, January 1, 2000, that finally quelled public fears.

It was a scary time for many people, but in North America, the actions taken to remedy the possible problems had unexpected benefits. Many businesses installed computer backup systems for critical files. The Y2K preparations had an impact August 14, 2003 during the Northeast Blackout of 2003. The previous activities had included the installation of new electrical generation equipment and systems, which allowed for a relatively rapid restoration of power in some areas.

It's also been suggested that on September 11, 2001, the New York infrastructure (including subways, phone service, and financial transactions) were able to continue operation because of the redundant networks established in the event of Y2K bug impact and the contingency plans devised by companies. The terrorist attacks and the following prolonged blackout to lower Manhattan had little effect on global banking systems and backup systems were activated, many of which had been established to deal with a possible complete failure of networks in the financial district on December 31, 1999. Had the emphasis on creating backup systems to deal with Y2K not occurred, much greater disruption to the economy might have happened.

There was hope in the midst of turmoil; there were opportunities to hold onto hope in spite of the fears for the future.

So worrying about the future isn't a new thing. Shucks, I worry about the future all the time. And it's getting worse as I get older, I tell ya; I find I'm more and more worried about the hereafter. Why just yesterday, I walked into my kitchen, and thought, "Now, what am I here after?" Yeah, worrying and wondering about the future is something we all have in common, even with the people in Luke's time.

So the apocalyptic cry, "The end is near!" is not a new cry by any means. It's no surprise that the first thing the people asked when Jesus made the prediction that the Temple would be destroyed is - 'when'?! And it's equally no surprise that he answers, "Many will come in my name and say, 'I am he!' and, 'The time is near!' - do not go after them." What I find fascinating in this text is that he never does answer their question, he never does say 'when'. Instead, he suggests a whole set of rather terrible and scary things are going to happen yet, "before all this occurs, they will arrest you and persecute you; they will hand you over to synagogues and prisons, and you will be brought before kings and governors because of my name. This will give you an opportunity - an opportunity, no less! - to testify!"

So in spite of doomsday predictions, in spite of hysteria, in spite of persecution, we're to hold on, have patience because we have opportunity - *and in that, is hope, the ultimate hope*. What does this kind of hope look like? Don't we need that kind of hope today? <u>Our</u> world is torn by war, <u>our</u> world sees people persecuted for their faith, <u>our</u> world sees innocent people brought before governments. Our world still sees doomsday cults. Not so long ago, in Russia, there was a doomsday cult in a cave siege. The group called itself the "True Russian Orthodox Church" and its members were waiting for the end of the world, which they expected to happen that May. They barricaded themselves inside a cave and threatened to blow it up!

Perhaps, sadly, it has always been so and remains so today. And yet, there are always *opportunities for hope* as well. As we prepare for Thanksgiving, it only seems fair to share a few *stories of hope* in the midst of peril and pain. I first heard these maybe 15 years ago. These stories are all true and I believe they go on today still; they're *stories of hope* in the midst of the storms that swirl around our lives.

[*pause*]

In war-torn Bosnia, small farming villages where Croats and Serbs had lived side by side for hundreds of years, were torn apart by the ethnic fighting going on. People who had been friends took up arms against each other. People who, in another time, looked out for each other, turned their backs on their neighbors' needs - if they weren't of the same ethnic group. But not all the time - not all the time.

There was a Croatian family that had a beautiful baby girl born to them in this nightmarish time. She was a quiet baby - peaceful and pretty. But there was no food for her! There was so little food for the parents, her mother couldn't even produce enough milk for the poor babe; it was clear that it would only be a matter of time before the little baby would die simply due to starvation. There was no hope of relief so long as the war went on. None of their Serbian neighbors could be expected to help - not now.

Yet one morning, as the mother comforted the poor little girl, she heard a knock

[*knock on something 3 times*]

at the door. Not knowing whether this would be friend or foe, she nervously opened the door a crack - and saw her neighbor - an elderly Serb farmer who had the only cow left in the village. He stood there in the cold grey dawn with a tin cup of milk in his hand. Silently, he held it out in the universal gesture of a gift. Almost in disbelief, she took it and he turned and slowly walked back to his home without saying a word.

Each morning - another cup of milk in silence and peaceful offering. That's virtually all the baby had yet it was enough for her to hold on - and survive. *There was hope* in the midst of war; there were opportunities to *hold onto hope* in spite of a future that seemingly offered none.

[*pause*]

In another town, in a different country and time - Minnesota during World War Two - a small community lived fitfully. It was a nice community, not very diverse, but caring, at least on the surface. There was just one German Jewish family in the small town; they were quiet and never gave anyone cause for concern. Although it was a time of blackouts and fears of enemy raiders possibly getting to our shores, in Minnesota in December, that seemed a distant fear to most folks. As a result, there was shock and fearful anger when someone threw a brick through the living room window of the small house where the Jewish family lived. All they had done was place menorah candles in the window, respecting their traditions. It was a light meant to be a beacon in the wilderness, but someone had torn their tradition apart stirring up fear in an already fearful time.

It didn't take long for the word to spread around the town; the family, once just on the edge of the community, now became even more isolated. What would happen next? Might somebody take the next step and firebomb their home? It had happened where they came from. Their fear was only exacerbated by their isolation. As the sun set the next evening, they didn't know what would happen in the night. They sat peering into the darkness, listening for every sound. Then something happened that broke through the darkness. The town began to light up - in spite of blackout demands!

First one house, then another, opened their front window curtains and placed - menorah candles - in the window! Candles lit to *shine hope* on a dark night. Over 800 homes in that small community had candles in their windows. Amazing light to *bring hope* in the darkness; opportunities to *hold onto hope* even over numbing fear.

    [*pause*]

A final example. In 1748, a young sailor on a stormy sea feared for his life as the ship might sink; he cried out to God for mercy. It became his opportunity to testify and he did - in this well-known hymn:

> Amazing Grace, how sweet the sound
> That saved a wretch like me...
> I once was lost but now am found;
> Was blind but now I see
>
> When we've been there ten thousand years
> Bright shining as the sea...
> We've no less days to sing God's praise
> Than when we first believed!

Jesus never answers the question of when; *he just gives us hope*. Even if our trials and tribulations last ten thousand years, *God will be our hope*! Amen!

[1] Boring, M. E. and Craddock, F. B., *The People's New Testament Commentary*, Westminster John Knox Press, Louisville, KY (2004), p. 264.

[2] Ibid., p. 94.

[3] Y2K references from: http://en.wikipedia.org/wiki/Y2K; 11/17/07, 6:32 am CST

Guess Who's Coming for Dinner?
Luke 14:15-24

15 One of the dinner guests, on hearing this, said to him, "Blessed is anyone who will eat bread in the kingdom of God!" 16 Then Jesus said to him, "Someone gave a great dinner and invited many. 17 At the time for the dinner he sent his slave to say to those who had been invited, 'Come; for everything is ready now.' 18 But they all alike began to make excuses. The first said to him, 'I have bought a piece of land, and I must go out and see it; please accept my regrets.' 19 Another said, 'I have bought five yoke of oxen, and I am going to try them out; please accept my regrets.' 20 Another said, 'I have just been married, and therefore I cannot come.' 21 So the slave returned and reported this to his master. Then the owner of the house became angry and said to his slave, 'Go out at once into the streets and lanes of the town and bring in the poor, the crippled, the blind, and the lame.' 22 And the slave said, 'Sir, what you ordered has been done, and there is still room.' 23 Then the master said to the slave, 'Go out into the roads and lanes, and compel people to come in, so that my house may be filled. 24 For I tell you, none of those who were invited will taste my dinner.'"

Choice is a funny thing, isn't it? Seems pretty easy, just choose what you like. You can choose to do something or choose not to; you can choose what clothes to wear or what not to wear! You can choose who to vote for and whether to get fries with that Big Mac; you can choose whether to stuff the turkey or not. I wonder, can you choose to be thankful? I think so but no matter what choices you make, there'll always be consequences. Isn't that the truth? You choose to eat that second or third piece of pumpkin pie come Thursday and there'll be consequences alright!

[pat stomach]

But I'd be thankful for them nonetheless!

I think our scripture for today is about choice and consequence too. Let's hear these words:

[read Luke 14:15-24]

See what I mean? The characters in this parable made choices. Some chose to make flimsy excuses to back out of a dinner invitation and some who didn't get invited at first got to come in the end. Sometimes you'd never guess who's gonna show up for dinner…or with dinner, for that matter.

Have I ever told you about my friend, Tommy? Tommy is an old friend of mine; I met him many years ago when I was doing some consulting work for a company over in Spencerville. Ever been to Spencerville? Sure you have - it's that little town on the way from here to there! It's a pretty little town with a nice town square and old streets lined with even older oak and maple trees. It was beautiful in the fall, but the leaves are all down by now. There's still the smell of burning leaves on the breeze; reminds me of when I was a child and we burned the fall leaves in our backyard.

I first met Tommy when he helped me with a flat tire, taking the tire over to Red's Garage without me even asking. He's thoughtful like that, at least he seems that way to me. Plenty other folks found him a little strange, maybe even slow, but I like him well enough. I usually run into Tommy at the Buttermilk Cafe where the owner, Elvira, watches over the comings and goings of the delightful assortment of characters any small town holds. You can see the whole square as you look out the front window of the Cafe where Elvira always displays a slice of pie along with a faded menu on a red checkerboard clothed table.

So, anyway, this time we were returning home after Thanksgiving and we ran into Tommy while we were getting gas in Concordia. He said he was returning home after visiting his grandfather who lives in a Nursing Home outside Wichita. We had some time, so we went to McDonald's, got some coffee and had a nice little visit. I asked how everything was down at the Buttermilk Cafe, how was Elvira and all her regulars; he said they were all fine although Elvira needed a little more help cleaning tables so he'd do that when she wasn't watching.

He mentioned how Javier Garcia had gotten all the wreaths and lights up for the annual Christmas Parade next weekend. Javier had been in town for a while, but it was good to see he'd gotten on with the County Agency as I knew their family needed all the help they could get.

Then I asked him, "Did you go down to Walmart for the Black Friday sales to get some good bargains?"

Now, at this, Tommy did one of the things that made some people think he was kind of slow. He just stared for a moment like this was a totally new thought to him, like he was from some other country or planet and had never heard of Walmart or Black Friday or even bargains! You couldn't really tell if he was looking at you or just slightly over your shoulder and it would seem like it would go on for several minutes; everything was suspended in time.

I'm sure it only lasted for seconds but it was disconcerting if you didn't know him.

Then he'd just smile and blink his eyes before speaking quietly.

"No, what would they have had down there to be thankful for that I haven't got right here? Oh, I went and got a turkey for Harvey to fix for the bridge people but 'Black Friday'? Seems like a kinda mean thing to call the day after Thanksgiving." he opined.

And then he smiled at me again. You know, I'd tell you what Tommy was wearing if I could ever remember it! His smile is what he wore best and what I remember the most.

"Besides, the really important thing is just a few weeks or so away. Baby Jesus is coming." Tommy said with evident relish.

I nodded, thinking about how I'd barely made it through Thanksgiving let alone was anywhere near ready for Christmas and here Tommy was already filled with anticipation and hope. We sipped some coffee, not saying anything, then I asked, "So, what were you thankful for this Thanksgiving, Tommy?"

"I'm thankful for Bennie and the Deuce!" he said positively.

He started out by telling me how Elvira at the Buttermilk Cafe closes for Thanksgiving - she visits her daughter's family on the other side of the state, I think primarily to see her two grandchildren, a boy and little sister. So Spencerville is pretty quiet. It's really quiet this year because Bennie and the Deuce are in the county lockup in Sheriff Hickersen's office! The Deuce is a smalltime hood, a conman and a no-good-Nick; Bennie is his sidekick. Bennie's not a bad dude, just kind of simple. He's tall and heavyset but really strong. No one's sure why he hangs around with the Deuce but there's some kind of symbiosis. The Deuce, who's always looking for an angle, uses Bennie all the time but still has some sort of loyalty to him.

But, like Tommy said, they're both in the slammer now. The Deuce got caught selling iPods that he and Bennie had 'picked up' somewhere, namely, off the Radio Shack in the little strip mall just west of town. They hadn't actually broken in, just happened to be around as the delivery truck was unloading! Due to the holidays, they couldn't be arraigned until next week so Sheriff Hickersen had to hold onto them. Thanksgiving in prison seemed like it would be a lonely affair.

Tommy said he chose to go visit Bennie and the Deuce. He didn't have anything to bring them except a can of cranberry sauce and a couple spoons. It was strange Tommy would even go because everyone assumed that that time Tommy's apartment was robbed, Bennie and the Deuce had something to do with it. But Tommy didn't judge them, or, maybe he forgave them; I don't know.

Of course, the Deuce wanted to know what was Tommy's angle - what was he going to get out of this visit? And if he wasn't getting anything then as far as the Deuce was concerned, he was just a chump.

But Bennie, normally pretty taciturn and quiet, told the Deuce to leave it alone; he was thankful for the cranberry sauce and for the visit. He told the Deuce, "Tommy never did nothing to us and he didn't have to do this. Thanks, Tommy."

Tommy was just glad to share with someone who needed a little love and compassion - that made it 'Thanksgiving' as far as he was concerned.

Another one of his over the shoulder gazes and then he spoke again. "And I'm thankful for you. And for Javier and Benny and Elvira and for my granddad and ... peanut butter!"

I laughed along with him saying, "Peanut Butter?! You like peanut butter?"

"No so much - but the squirrels sure do! It's their 'turkey and gravy' on Thanksgiving and they'll think it's a fine Christmas gift too. Them and the birds look so pretty against the trees and fallen leaves still on the ground, I can't imagine anything much more beautiful... well, except for the candles on Christmas Eve shining on the manger."

Tommy smiled and lifted his eyebrows conspiratorially at me and said, "If you look just right, you can see God all over the place."

    [*pause*]

After the quiet wore off, Tommy hopped up and said, "Gee, it was great to see you but I've gotta run, Red's got an old tire fixed for Elvira and I promised to get back in time to put it on her car so she could drive to church tomorrow!"

With better clarity from the caffeine and greater hope from Tommy, we headed across the bridge and through the woods to go home, thankful all the way!

Happy Thanksgiving, everyone! Amen!

What if?
Mark 6:32-44

32 And they went away in the boat to a deserted place by themselves. 33 Now many saw them going and recognized them, and they hurried there on foot from all the towns and arrived ahead of them. 34 As he went ashore, he saw a great crowd; and he had compassion for them, because they were like sheep without a shepherd; and he began to teach them many things. 35 When it grew late, his disciples came to him and said, "This is a deserted place, and the hour is now very late; 36 send them away so that they may go into the surrounding country and villages and buy something for themselves to eat." 37 But he answered them, "You give them something to eat." They said to him, "Are we to go and buy two hundred denarii[a] worth of bread, and give it to them to eat?" 38 And he said to them, "How many loaves have you? Go and see." When they had found out, they said, "Five, and two fish." 39 Then he ordered them to get all the people to sit down in groups on the green grass. 40 So they sat down in groups of hundreds and of fifties. 41 Taking the five loaves and the two fish, he looked up to heaven, and blessed and broke the loaves, and gave them to his disciples to set before the people; and he divided the two fish among them all. 42 And all ate and were filled; 43 and they took up twelve baskets full of broken pieces and of the fish. 44 Those who had eaten the loaves numbered five thousand men.

In keeping with our focus on Black History Month, we'll hear about George Washington Carver this morning: George Washington Carver was an African American scientist and educator. He was born into slavery yet went on to become one of the most prominent scientists and inventors of his time.

He was most likely born into slavery in 1864 in Diamond, Missouri; one of many children born to Mary and Giles, an enslaved couple owned by Moses Carver. A week after his birth, he was kidnapped along with his sister and mother by raiders from Arkansas. The three were later sold in Kentucky. Among them, only the infant George was located by an agent of Moses Carver and returned to Missouri.

Moses and his wife, Susan, decided to keep George and his brother James at their home after that time, raising and educating the two boys. Susan Carver taught him to read and write since no local school would accept black students. The search for knowledge would remain a driving force for the rest of his life. As a young man, he left the Carver home to travel to a school for black children 10 miles away. It was at this point that George, who had always identified himself as "Carver's George" first came to be known as "George

Carver." He attended a series of schools before receiving his diploma at Minneapolis High School in Minneapolis, Kansas.

Accepted to Highland College in Highland, Kansas, he was denied admittance once college administrators learned of his race. So instead of attending classes, he homesteaded a claim, where he conducted biological experiments and compiled a geological collection. While interested in science, Carver was also interested in the arts. In 1890, he began studying art and music at Simpson College in Iowa, developing his painting and drawing skills through sketches of botanical samples. His obvious aptitude for drawing the natural world prompted a teacher to suggest that Carver enroll in the botany program at the Iowa State Agricultural College.

Through undergraduate and graduate studies, Carver established his reputation as a brilliant botanist. After George graduated from Iowa State, Booker T. Washington, the founder of the historically black Tuskegee Institute, hired him to run the school's agricultural department in 1896. Carver's work at the helm of the Tuskegee Institute's agricultural department included groundbreaking research on plant biology, much of which focused on the development of new uses for crops including peanuts, sweet potatoes, soybeans and pecans. Carver's inventions include hundreds of products, including more than 300 from peanuts (milk, plastics, paints, dyes, cosmetics, medicinal oils, soap, ink, wood stains), 118 from sweet potatoes (molasses, postage stamp glue, flour, vinegar and synthetic rubber) and even a type of gasoline.

At the time, cotton production was on the decline in the South, and overproduction of a single crop had left many fields exhausted and barren. Carver suggested planting peanuts and soybeans, both of which could restore nitrogen to the soil, along with sweet potatoes. While these crops grew well in southern climates, there was little demand. It was Carver's inventions and research that solved this problem. This all helped to stabilize the livelihoods of people, many former slaves who had backgrounds not unlike Carver's own. The education of African American students at Tuskegee contributed directly to economic stabilization among blacks. Carver's efforts made it possible for folks to survive, to put food on their table and raise their children.

In George Carver's words: "It is not the style of clothes one wears, neither the kind of automobile one drives, nor the amount of money one has in the bank that counts. These mean nothing. It is simply service that measures success."

I believe George Washington Carver would especially appreciate our text, Mark 6:32-44.

[*read text*]

This text, about the feeding of the 5000, is one we all know and love. I mean, feeding everyone is part of Disciples of Christ DNA and specially our DNA. Look! There's the table right in the middle of worship! Even the children know how important feeding people is to us. You know, I heard there was a teacher who invited the students to bring in something that represented their individual faith traditions for show and tell.

A little Jewish boy showed everyone his brimless cap telling them, "This is my yarmulke - we wear it when we're worshipping as a sign of humility and honor for YHWH - God."

Next, a Catholic girl stood and showed a necklace with beads saying, "This is my rosary, it helps me keep track of my prayers."

Then the Disciples of Christ kid held up his traditional faith element saying, "This - is a casserole dish…"

So, yeah, we know about feeding people!

[*pause*]

All kidding aside, there are a few things that should be discussed as we unpack this well-known story. This is an example of a category of stories called miracle stories. In order to interpret these stories, we need to understand a few general characteristics. First, miracle stories were part of the ancient world, both religious and pagan.

"In the Hellenistic world, miracles belong to the realm of the possible and constitute an accepted part of the worldview of most people. That worldview understood that the world is not a closed system of nature that God must interrupt in a supernatural way in order to act. Rather, the world functions as it normally does because God wills it such; God can occasionally will it otherwise."[1]

As a result, the facticity of miracles was generally accepted. Their meaning is what was debated.

"Miracle stories in the Bible and in the Gospels in particular, are not primarily evidential, not for proving a point. Neither are they primarily manifestations of people's faith. They do not typically happen as the reward for someone's faith; the message is not "If you believe well enough, you will have miracles too or, if you don't have miracles, you do not have enough faith." It's not that at all.

In the Gospels, the miraculous is an eschatological category. Eschatology is the study of end times. Thus the telling of miracle stories about Jesus is one way of claiming that, in him, God's kingdom has appeared. The miracle stories call the reader to decide whether Jesus Christ represents God's eschatological act for our salvation. They do not necessarily call for belief or unbelief in the literal truth of the story."[2]

In a nutshell: In the ancient world, most people believe miracles happen; they don't question their facticity. The question is what they mean. In the Gospels, the miracle stories point to God's kingdom appearing in Jesus; the Christ event is the eschatology, i.e., end time, event. In this respect, they're like Jesus' parables, "The kingdom of God is like..."

These stories have been interpreted in a variety of ways over the millennia but rather than going through all the interpretation possibilities, let's jump right into our miracle story for today - the feeding of the 5000.

This story is unique in that it is the only miracle story about Jesus to appear in all four Gospels. The image of Jesus who feeds the hungry was central to early Christian faith. In fact, one of the earliest Christian symbols was that of the fish. Here are a few examples from early church mosaics from the 3rd and 6th centuries. [*show slides of fish mosaics*] These reminders of the miracle of the fishes and loaves are powerful images pointing to the messianic banquet described in various scriptures, for example, Psalm 23, "You prepare a table a table before me - my cup overflows..", Matt 22, "The kingdom of God may be compared to a king who gave a wedding banquet for his son.." and in the celebration of the Lord's Supper which we know so well.

All four start with Jesus and a multitude of people. There's a concern for how they will eat. In Matthew, Mark and Luke, the disciples suggest letting them go to the surrounding towns to buy their own food. John turns it around having Jesus ask rhetorically, "Where are we to buy bread for these people to eat?" The disciples complain it will cost too much.

Then, and this is the same translation in Matthew, Mark and Luke, Jesus replies, "You give them something to eat." Clearly, we are to hear that being directed to us as well. "You give them something to eat." But what can we give? Common to all 4 versions, there are 5 loaves and 2 fish, which Jesus blesses and shares - just as we do today in communion - a celebration of the eucharistic feast - everyone is filled, satisfied and there's 12 baskets left over!

The miracle is done by God. The disciples don't do it, the people don't do it. It makes no difference if the people believe in Jesus, it doesn't matter if they have strong, little or no faith, it doesn't matter whether they're Jewish or Gentile - God still miraculously feeds everyone!

Just a thought - have you ever seen the bread and the cup run out around this table? Is it not clear now that when pastor Kelley invites everyone to the table each week, she invites everyone with no distinction about where you're from or what you believe, all are welcome - *just like this miracle story?*

[*pause*]

Pretty cool, huh?!

But still… where'd the bread and fish come from? Now this gets interesting, at least to me! Matthew, Mark and Luke don't say where the food comes from but John does. He has Andrew say, "There is a boy here who has 5 barley loaves and 2 fish…" A friend of mine from Seminary days, Rev. Georgeann Peck, told me this story…

[*move away from pulpit to tell 'The Boy with 2 fish and 5 loaves Story'*]

Story synopsis: A local boy and his friends hear about Jesus and decide to follow the crowds to see what it's all about - it's plainly too exciting for young boys to miss, almost like the circus coming to town. He tells his mom what he's going to do and before he can run out the door, she makes him tell her what he's going to do, when he'll come home, who he's going with - I guess moms in Jesus' time were pretty much the same as my mom when I was an inquisitive, on the go kid - and she packs up a basket with some bread and a couple fish and tells him to make sure and eat and that he can share with his friends if he needs to.

Off the boy and his friends go. They follow the crowds down to the lakeshore. The crowds have been there awhile and the sun is now starting down the sky. Even the rambunctious boys are getting tired. But the boy with the fish and loaves had wriggled his way to the front of the crowd so he could actually see Jesus so he and his basket were right there when Jesus said, "How will we feed all these people?" And he remembered his mom saying, "You can share if you need to… she said it was okay to share…"

Later, as the sun hit the horizon, the boy got back home. He was dusty and dirty and his mom asked how the day was and he told her how Jesus blessed his bread and fish and how everyone ate and how it was amazing. She interrupted, "But did you get any to eat? I told you to eat…". The boy interrupted back, "But mom, you said I could share…"

[*move back to pulpit*]

She gave him permission to share. **What if** that's all it took? Just his mom saying, it's ok - you can share. And **what if** we look at the Gospels through the lens of permission? Isn't that what Jesus offers over and over? **What if** we see Jesus' statement "Come and follow me" as permission? It's okay, I'll make you fishers of men…

And **what if** the sermon on the mount is viewed as a series of permissions? I give you permission to love your enemy, to give your cloak, to go the extra mile.

And **what if** he gave permission to the woman at the well to share her story? Your story's important and you're important; it's okay for you to give me water and tell your village.

And **what if** he gave Peter permission to forgive over and over, 70 times 7? It's okay Peter, you can forgive just as much as you're forgiven!

And **what if** he gave the disciples permission to feed the people? It's okay, go ahead and feed them; what have you got?

And **what if** Susan Carver was just giving young George permission to study and learn? It's okay - you can go to school; you can learn to read and write.

What if - we read the gospels through the lens of permission giving? Not permission to do whatever we want to do but to stop doing the things that hurt us, that hold us apart, that keep us from becoming who God means for us to be?

Jesus gives us permission to follow him, he gives us permission to give away sack lunches, permission to house and feed Family Promise families, support CONCERN, Agape` and others, gives us permission to wash each other's feet, gives us permission to forgive over and over, gives us permission to love others as he loves us!

Just like the mother who loved her young son and gave him permission to share 5 loaves and 2 fish if he needed to.

What if - you - were given permission? Imagine the miracles God could do! Amen!

---

[1] Boring, M. E. and Craddock, F. B., The People's New Testament Commentary, Westminster John Knox Press, Louisville, KY (2004), p. 43.

[2] Ibid., p. 44.

Sermons in Outline Format

The following sermons are in outline format suitable for being printed in 2-column landscape mode on a standard 8.5 x 11" page. It may require reducing font size but they will fit on one side of a standard sheet of paper. Folded in half and taped it on the inside cover of my Bible, the outline thus allowed me flexibility to move around among the congregation.

The form provided plenty of room to improvise and extemporize rather than simply reading a prepared speech. I believe these few examples are clear enough for anyone to flesh out for their own time and place.

Spiritual Freedom
Gal 5:1, 13-25

1. My favorite verse - 5:1, "For freedom, Christ has set us free." What does Paul mean by 'freedom'? What were they trapped, enslaved, or ruled by back then? What did the word translated as 'freedom' mean?

2.. In Paul's time, strict social stratification and a patronage system for interaction between strata; for example, this controlled:

- who you could date, marry - even hang out with

- where and what you ate

- jobs you could get

3. Pagan religion was very ritualized; Jewish religious ritual was defined by Holiness and Cleanliness codes - if you didn't do this right, you couldn't go to worship.

- *it sure is nice we don't have rules and codes, isn't it?!*

4. So what did 'freedom' mean for Paul? Greek - *eleutheros* - unrestrained (to go at pleasure), not a slave or exempt (from obligation or liability), at liberty.

    and 'to free'

eleutheroo - to liberate, to exempt (from moral, ceremonial or mortal liability), deliver - make free.

5. Clearly, he means freedom from the rules and codes that everyone had to follow but he also means exemption from the holiness and cleanliness codes - they don't justify you or make you innocent.

- Christ doesn't set us free for nothing - it's so we, too, can be free!

    Free to... what??

6. This is where it gets interesting - this is a real paradigm shift, a real difference in our world view. For Paul, this is nothing less than seeing that in Christ, there is no longer Jew or greek, male or female, slave or free...

It's not that now, you can't put folks in categories, decide where and who you can eat with, etc., etc. - *it's that you don't have to... you're free!*

[*pause*]

7. Now, the rest of today's text begins to make sense - the fruits of the Spirit discussion.

8. Have these things ever 'ruled' you? idolatry, jealousy, anger, dissensions, envy, carousing...?

Did you ever notice how we have to think about these? We'll spend hours planning and plotting - how to get it to work out our way...

But it sure is nice we don't have rules and codes like they did, isn't it?!

9. And did you ever notice that you don't have to think much about love, joy, peace, patience, kindness, generosity, faithfulness, gentleness, self-control - they just happen?

10. What Paul wants his listeners to know - today just as much as 'back in the day'... it's not that now we can't be idolatrous, angry, jealous, drunk, etc., etc. - it's that we don't have to! (reference verse 5:12)

For freedom, Christ has set us free!   Amen!

My God, Your God
Acts 11:1-18

1. When I went to seminary long ago, I 'knew' God was a progressive liberal who loved everyone - everyone. And I felt sorry for those who seemed to have a different God - a much more conservative God, bound by fundamental, literalist readings.

- I had my God and they, seemingly, had their God.

'Those' people were surely in for a big surprise, I thought!

- Of course, in the end, it was me who got a surprise, too.

2. Take this text from Acts. It must be important; the author repeats it twice in the space of two chapters. This is important enough that we should take a closer look at the whole story [*go back to chap. 10*]

- 'Those' people weren't who we thought they were!

Apparently, God talks to 'them'; works through 'them'! What was God thinking, talking to 'them'? Is this a trick? Everybody knows 'they're' unclean, even abominations!

    [*pause*]

3. Tommy Story...

- Met him in Spencerville, that little town on the way from here to there... - retell story about picking up dishes at the Buttermilk Cafe`... Tommy's - different, some even think a little slow, but Tommy seems to know everyone.

- I see him at church - sometimes - so I asked him why - he says he goes somewhere each Sunday - sees God everywhere he goes.
- I diss on 'those' people - maybe the ones who say if you don't believe what they believe, you're going to Hell - if you're woman preacher, if you're gay, if you're Muslim, Jewish, Buddhist... whatever...

Tommy looks up and quietly said:

- *What part of God do you not see in 'those' people?*

[pause]

- *wait a sec... does God have parts??*

4. No - God doesn't have parts! God is totally simple, Thomas Aquinas 'proved' that in his masterwork, *Summa Theologica*, a long time ago. God can't be a collection of parts - you can't get a piece of God; you can only get the whole thing.

5. But we like to make our world into pieces: 'either-or', 'us-them', 'black-white', 'gay-straight', 'christian-muslim', and on and on.

6. But apparently, God sees the world as 'we', 'you (plural)' - throughout the Bible, the stories tend to show 'both-and' as opposed to 'either-or', Jesus' whole ministry is about God's kindom of 'both-and'...

7. So we can go through our lives, fastidiously avoiding the 'unclean' like Peter before this odd vision, or we can listen to Tommy who echoes Peter's conclusions, "If then God gave them the same gift that he gave us when we believed in the Lord Jesus Christ, who am I that I could hinder God?" vs. 18:17

- *What part of God do you not see in those people?* Amen!

Shouting Stones
Luke 19:28-40

1. Two entries into Jerusalem - Romans enter on the other side - fanfare/war horses, etc.

Comparison of Gospel versions - although each has its bias, they're all consistent that Jesus set it up - that he knew what he was doing and that it was in the face of the authorities.

- Palm Sunday is Jesus basically saying, "You're not the boss of me - or anybody else!" Pretty passionate, huh?

2. Passion - what was Jesus' passionate about? The kingdom of God!

3. Who else has said this:

> Martyrs under Romans
>
> Paul, Peter, Stephen, etc. Disciples
>
> Martin Luther, Martin Luther King, Jr., Oscar Romero
>
> Thomas Campbell, Alexander Campbell, Barton Stone - all 'excommunicated' from Presbyterians etc. etc.

4. That's why the Pharisees are scared - Jesus is passionate about *God's* kingdom - and this puts him against the Roman Imperial forces and the Emperor himself! They're scared the powers that be will come down heavy on them - hey, it's happened before! It still happens today!

- protestors in Iran, China, Tibet, Myanmar, Sudan, etc., etc.

5. But what are we passionate about? I'm just not that political - I don't get passionate about that sort of thing, do you?

6. For example, the healthcare debate - I don't understand it all, I haven't said much about it - all this talk about being forced into the program... Now, maybe it would be good for those who can get insurance to have the ability to opt out - but what about those who haven't got any choice at all? Is that the way God's kingdom is? Some can have it and some can't??

[*start getting louder*...] but some of "those" people are part of us - they're the people I try to pastor, to care for... they're the ones who can't afford their meds, they're the ones who I drive to appointments and to the ER when they're too sick to just tough it out. They don't get any care - because they can't even have an option of any kind! And they're my friends!! God's children! They'd never be treated this way in God's kingdom!

[*pause*] - but who're you gonna listen to?... who can you trust?

7. Baptism - who's your Lord? In baptism, we acknowledge and affirm Jesus as Lord:

- Do you believe in God, the Father, Creator of all things?
- And in Jesus Christ, God's only Son, Redeemer of the world?
- And in the Holy Spirit, who unites the Church in love?

I do! - Except when I don't - when I let the "powers that be" say how things will be rather than sticking to the statement of my baptism - that God is in charge! The God of heaven and earth! The God of all creation!

8. I wish I was as passionate as all those I mentioned earlier- maybe I am in some ways - maybe you are too. And maybe today - Palm Sunday, a day that stands out in Jesus' ministry as a day of being passionate about God's kingdom - will inspire me and you to be more passionate for God's kingdom too.

- there will be suffering... but that's part of the meaning of 'passion'.

9. Was Jesus passionate? There were two processions into Jerusalem on this Palm - this Passion - Sunday. Which one will you be in? Which will you be passionate about?

Jesus tells those worried Pharisees - even the whole of creation is passionate - if we stay silent, even the stones will shout out - to the empires and the corporations and PACS and domination systems - "You're not the boss of us - God is!"   Amen!

Sin In A Nutshell
Luke 4:1-11

1. Sin. Who knew such a teeny, tiny work could give us so much grief! Our text doesn't mention sin but I think we'd all agree that Satan is tempting Jesus to sin so I guess we'll have to deal with it. So hold onto that thought, we'll end up back at 'sin'...

2. But for now, let's dig a little further into this temptation stuff.

3. First, there are some trigger images - '40 days' this immediately evokes Israel's time in the wilderness during the exodus. '40 days' - the time of Moses up on Mt. Sinai

Those events didn't turn out so good tho - the people gave in to temptation...

So the audience knows this and is being purposefully led to that comparison - the story isn't just Jesus' temptation - it's about our temptations too.

4. First, there's the temptation to turn stones into bread. This is about physical desires. Certainly, feeding the hungry is a good thing...

- Second, there's the temptation to rule the whole world. This is about power and control. Imagine the good Jesus could do if he was in control...

- Third, the temptation to test God. This is about *being* God. If you are God-like, why not use it?

- In each case, Jesus replies with scripture from Deuteronomy - all about reverence for God; perhaps more telling, Jesus does NOT resort to miraculous powers but relies on God - it's *Satan who uses miraculous powers*...

5. First and foremost, Jesus stays true to God rather than taking care of himself. Second, he stays human - and shows it's demonic to use miraculous powers!

6. Soooo... have you ever been tempted like this? Yeah, me too. We ALL fail at these temptations - we eat too much and at the expense of others, we all think, "If I were in charge, I'd fix that healthcare system...", and we all have wished for miraculous powers, the desire to heal a loved one, for example.

In all of these temptations, we have valued ourselves over and above our relationship with God and Jesus.

Sometimes, this is easy and obvious to see - take the recent events [*murder case*] ... temptations mess up your life!

Sometimes, it's a thought or attitude and sometimes, we think we can keep it secret - but whatever 'it' is, it separates us from God.

>[*pause*]

7. I got a phone call this week from an old friend - Tommy...

[*Tommy's in south Texas, works at a homeless center and told me I could share our discussion. I told him about this week's text and he mentioned a program he's working on to help folks addicted to internet porn...it's all of these temptations wrapped up in one place! Stories of broken families, STDs,*]

8. So what's that got to do with us? All those temptations are right here in Grand Island, NE. In a nutshell, 'sin' is when we give in to the temptations. Sin - right here in River City, so to speak!

9. But so is Jesus. You see, Jesus didn't choose to take the devil up, no, he chose to be human and be faithful to God - just to be with us and help us repent and rely on God, too.

10. There's so, so much more to say about sin - the way we participate in corporate sin, the way sometimes something that's wrong might not be sin.

- But this text tells us Jesus is there for us - he won't abandon us to make it easy on himself, no, he won't fall for the temptation!

And that, is very good news! Amen.

www.ingramcontent.com/pod-product-compliance
Lightning Source LLC
Chambersburg PA
CBHW052138110526
44591CB00012B/1767